There is Life Beyond the Grave! – I Shall Not Die But Live

By

Crystal Yvonne Dixon

This book is a work of non-fiction.
The events and situations are true.

ISBN: 1-4107-8583-1 (e-book)
ISBN: 1-4107-8584-X (Paperback)

This book is printed on acid free paper.

1stBooks – rev. 08/06/03

TABLE OF CONTENTS

THERE IS LIFE BEYOND THE GRAVE!
– PART 1

It's spring 2003 in Baltimore City and I am reflecting on just how good God has been to me. There comes a time you must tune everything out and meditate on Jesus, and how worthy He is. If it had not been for the power and hand of God in my life I would not be here. It's because of Him I have faith and hope. I am writing this book in hopes that someone reading will feel that God loves them and that what God says and promises is faithful and true. I am going on 33 years old this year in 2003 and the more test and trials I go through the more I see that God loves me. I am hoping that my testimony will strengthen and encourage somebody rather they are in the body of Christ or just somebody that really need that extra push to hold on.

Where do I start? I have been born in Baltimore City, Maryland as Crystal Yvonne Sweeney to Joan and Willie Sweeney on August 21, 1970. My parents were very young when they got married with my mother being 18 years old and my father being 21 years old, however they dated years before that. I have a sister that is 12 years younger who is now 21 years old this year, Endeara Joan Sweeney, who is my only sibling. I always wished I had more brothers and sisters and I think Endeara feels this way also. Endeara's smart as a whip. My mother taught her how to read as a baby and taught her home schooling. Even now I am happy at how she has handled her life with maturity. She is so hard on herself and my parents put too much pressure on her. I graduated from Paul Laurence Dunbar Sr. High School with honors ranking #4 out of 150 students in 1988. Sam Cassell who is now in the NBA was in my graduating class but I never got a chance to see him play basketball in high school because at the time my parents and Jehovah's Witnesses would not allow it. I have 4 children ages 7 months (Joy Elizabeth Dixon), 4 years old (Linda Ann Bey), 7 years old (India Yvonne Sweeney-Bey) and 12 years old (Joshua Aaron Sweeney). I got married May 21, 2002 at the court house. I have 2 years college under my belt as a graduate at the Community College of Baltimore County, formerly Dundalk Community College, in 1995 with an Office Supervision Certificate. I was raised Jehovah's Witness from birth by both parents and both sides of my family are strongly in Jehovah's Witnesses. I became a saved Christian in 1993 when I gave my hand to the preacher and my heart to Christ. I was baptized as a Jehovah's Witness at age 14 and at age 18 got excommunicated. I got baptized so many times seeking God for myself it's ridiculous. I was baptized as a Moslem as a Moorish American, changing my name and Joshua's name to Bey, seeking God and getting involved in the Moslem faith over a man. I got baptized at United Baptist Church where the pastor is Rev. Carl J. Solomon after attending New Life discipleship classes in a Pentacostal Holiness church, Kingdom Worship Center, where the pastor is Ralph Dennis, where I met my now spiritual mom and close friend. My spiritual mother taught the New Life Class and so she recommended that I get baptized at United Baptist Church. I stayed at United Baptist Church from 1993 to 2000 and left to go to First Apostolic Faith Church where I got baptized in the name of Jesus and got the baptism of the Holy Spirit. I never became a member at First Apostolic Faith Church but that is also where I met my husband. My entire Christian faith walk was a long process. When I got baptized in the Holy Spirit I knew I had the Comforter and God inside me no matter what anybody said or did. For years I was a member in United Baptist Church still fornicating, still compromising, and tore up from the floor up! Once I went to First Apostolic Faith Church where Bishop Cornelius Showell is pastor, my life changed. I will never forget what happened. It was 2000 when Hurricane Floyd hit Baltimore and I came running in the church with jeans and an old

2

shirt. Hurricane Floyd was terrible hitting Baltimore. I was coming from a job interview out in Hunt Valley, Maryland on the lightrail and bus. When I got near my home, I ran into a senior citizen building and just as I got into the sliding glass door, the wind knocked the entire glass door. I got home finally praising and thanking God. At the time I was suffering so much financially and emotionally, I was getting a stipend check of $77 a month from the rental office for my BGE and that was all of the income I had each month. I couldn't get food stamps or public assistance for myself, I was getting Meals on Wheels at the time, I was losing weight severely, and sick as a dog, but that day when the hurricane hit and I found a letter under the door to pick up my $77 check from the rental office, I was in need of a breakthrough and knew I was on borrowed time and should have been dead that day. God was faithful to me. I was not paying any rent for almost two years because the management changed my rent to $0 rent due to the fact I had no income and I was on Section 8 housing. Every time I tried to work or get income on my own working temporary agencies, the assignments were short term and not enough. So I decided to go to church that night at First Apostolic Faith Church after my neighbor invited me. They were having a revival and alter call. My heart was already open and ready for deliverance. Then Bishop Showell, who is a very tall big man, laid hands on me and I starting talking in tongues. I didn't know what in world was going on and got scared at first because this was not my flesh talking and I had no control of it. The tears were flowing and I was on the floor. I left out the sanctuary and one of the mothers of the church came to me and said to go back in the line and get my deliverance. She saw I was scared and it was new to me. I walked from the church to my home worshipping the Lord talking in tongues for the first time. Since then I have a deeper personal relationship with Jesus. I don't have to run to a pastor or anybody for comfort or help. There were times I wanted to die and throw in the towel but God would stir up the Holy Ghost and put a song of praise in me. Next thing I knew I was ready to kick the devil butt and be the soldier of the Lord God predestined me to be. Well, that's my general background information.

It's May 2, 2003 and I just got my echocardiogram. I had been dealing with stress all week long. I had to contact the Baltimore City

Health Dept. to come to my home about a 7 month old severe rodent problem in my apartment and finally they gave management a citation and fine of $100. Thank you, Jesus! I mean it pays not to give up. I was dealing with that along with the fact my 3 children: Joshua, Linda, and India are in foster homes and I have been fighting for custody. The child custody issue is a book all by itself and I will talk about that in more detail but right now I want to give God the glory. I mean the devil was really trying to attack me hard. I kept getting negative reports and got so discouraged that I was thinking about suicide. Easter past and my children were still not home. I had Joy all dressed up in her first Easter outfit, all pretty in peach and white. My husband was not with me from 4/12/03 until Easter, which also dampened my spirits a little since it was our first Easter as a married couple and Joy's first. On 4/12/03 my parents and extended family got the chance to see Joshua without me which really hurt. I contacted Joshua's psychologist, Dr. Donna Dryer from MENTOR (refer to www. thementornetwork.com for information about the program. CPS assigned Joshua to MENTOR without any court order by a judge or allowing me to contest by a trial hearing) who without any court order by a judge took it upon herself to block visits allowing only extended family, stating Joshua is a sensitive child. Visits had been blocked since 1999 and my son has been in the foster care system since 1998. MENTOR took photos professionally done and gave them to my mother and extended family. That hurt bad. So when Holy Week 2003 came I was a mess but I kept going to Palm Sunday, Good Friday, and Easter service with my heart open and wounded. By the time I went to First Apostolic Faith Church for early morning Easter Service, I praised the Lord until I couldn't any more. Yes, people looked at me like a nut but I closed my eyes and the spirit of the Lord moved. If I didn't worship and praise God I would have lost it. There is a blessing in the praise. I learned this Easter that God puts you in situations that seem tough not for yourself or for anybody else to take credit, but for somebody else to get empowered and for God to get full credit and praise. My spiritual mother called me and said that the devil just wants me to shut up and that I have something God wants me to say to the body of Christ. I went into a high praise then. Then I got an email from North Carolina for housing after I did an AOL search, and I got another good report that they would help me. I was really happy then because management who got the citation came into my home telling me that they wanted me to move from my 2 bedroom apartment to one bedroom. God is a god of promotion and increase!

Now I will talk about my child custody because it is still hard on me but proof that there's still victory in Jesus and hope beyond the grave. When I say hope beyond the grave, I am talking about issues that are meant to take you out in your spirit physically, emotionally, mentally, financially, and any other way to kill your faith in God. There is a God that is concerned and promises to never leave or forsake you. There is a God that heals the oppressed full of compassion. The entire Child Protective Service matter really started in 1996 because my son is special needs and due to the fact I didn't have support systems as a single parent. Joshua's father was not in the picture. My parents played part time grandparents and would not even call Joshua. All they were concerned was about me coming back to being a Jehovah's Witness. When I would allow Joshua to stay with them, my mother would have Joshua bring back literature and drawings she made of Joshua playing with lions in the "paradise". Of course, this would upset me, because I would have Joshua in Sunday school, and teach him true Christian Bible principles. When I had India and Linda, I had them by two different fathers. I should have waited and got married before having children. Here I was kicked out Jehovah's Witnesses faith at age 18, homeless, and disowned by my parents and family. So I created my own family and what I thought was support. CPS got involved in 1996 and made the claim unsubstantiated because they didn't have enough evidence against me and they did an in-house review expunging the record in 1996. Then in 1998, I asked social services for assistance for furniture, housing, and daycare. The DSS worker accused me of neglect when I asked them for assistance. The woman didn't take photos of my home and the children. My son damaged the furniture so badly and I had a severe rodent problem then that I had to get rid of the furniture. My son was in a school bus accident and so his behavior went from good to bad to the point India was not safe. Joshua injured India while I was in the kitchen cooking and CPS blamed me. India's foot was burned by accident and I didn't take her to the ER. I did First Aid on my own because the burn was not bad for the ER. I took both children to the nurse practitioner that week and that's when they took my children. My appointment was for 11am at Johns Hopkins Hospital and Joshua went into his behavior tantrums. We waited hours before being seen, which now thinking about it, I should have left and went home since it was Joshua's birthday too. By the time the nurse practitioner came I was in tears, tired, and Joshua was uncontrollable. My children never had a pediatrician since birth and the nurse practitioner was new. It was Joshua's 7 year old check up. I told them about Joshua's behavior at home, that I needed him to be on medication like Ritalin, and hospitalized like he was in 1996 for his behavior. I was told to leave to get lunch and when I came back I told them about India's foot. They later accused me of severely burning India's foot and never contacted the police or took photos of the burn. They called CPS while I got lunch and snatched India out my arms, handcuffed me, and put me in the psychiatric part of the ER overnight. I wasn't told where my children were for weeks. CPS and the courts had a shelter hearing without giving me any notice. I was never given the chance to have a trial to contest the initial allegations and was forced to obey CPS. Then to set it off, I never had any criminal charges pressed on me by Johns Hopkins Hospital or CPS for any of their allegations which I thought was going to happened since I was handcuffed in the hospital by police. I had the imprint of the handcuffs on my arms for the entire week. The State placed the case in the juvenile court system as a civil case for child neglect like the children were property and I was never deemed liable by a judge of neglect from 1998 to 2003. In the fall of 1998 I was told by the master judge to comply with CPS without the judge telling me what my Constitutional rights were and the public defender at the time would not appeal or request a trial. From the fall of 1998 to June 1999 I was told I had to comply with the CPS service plan which is a contract with biased stating all the ropes they want you to do to get your children back. The contract was not viewed by the public defender and I was not told that I had the legal right not to sign anything without a trial. I completed everything under duress and ignorance. The CPS worker was Aronda Okojie from the fall of 1998 to fall 1999. I asked for another worker and got Rita Animashaun from 1999 to 2003. Both of them were deceptive and manipulative with the case. The CPS service plan was drawn up by Aronda Okojie. Visits were arranged based upon the foster care parents and the worker's convenience and they would bring one child and not the other. A judge never enforced how CPS should arrange the visits, and the public defender never contested the fact I had supervised visits without a trial and my lawyer never demanded regular weekly visits. I would have only one visit a month that were only one hour long despite the fact the service plan stated biweekly visits. I finished parenting classes by May 1999, I had to comply to a psychiatric evaluation arranged by Aronda Okojie at Johns Hopkins Hospital, I had to comply to giving my medical records to CPS which violated my right to privacy, I had to undergo supervised visits at CPS site that was not court ordered by the judge, and I was treated like a criminal instead of innocent until proven by a judge guilty or liable of the allegations. By June 1999, I was told that I had to wait until Linda was born and that I had to go through another psychological evaluation. My public defender, Grace Kilchenstein, who was my second attorney since October 1998, stated that she personally didn't think I should have my children until I gave birth to Linda. I contested her opinion and wanted a trial and appeal and she ignored everything. CPS has a rule that if they have the children in foster care over 15 months they can petition to terminate parental rights. So Aronda Okojie, the CPS worker, in 1998 was so neglectful on the case that it caused the 15 month rule to fall into place, ignoring due process and fundamental Constitutional right to a speedy trial rather civil or criminal case. From June 1998 when they took Joshua and India up to June 1999, that was 12 months wasted by the CPS worker, and months I didn't have to comply to anything without a trial contesting all initial allegations. So September 1999 was the 15 months and was when the CPS termination rights rule started. I was forced to go through another psychological evaluation in which my public defender, Grace Kilchenstein, the same person that stated I should wait until I have Linda, refused to demand limitations on the number of evaluations without a trial. I had Linda taken from me under the stipulation that I had to be under 24/7 supervision under my parents' home and live there, which was difficult being that they are Jehovah's Witnesses. My parents knew I was under this CPS stipulation that was not court ordered by the judge or viewed by my attorney and so my parents didn't support me. Linda got ill and when I had to take her to the hospital my mother would not take her and I was under their supervision in their home. So CPS took Linda at the hospital and I got physically ill. CPS falsely alleged that I volunteerily put Linda in the system. Linda was born July 20, 1999 and I had her taken from me in August. I had to undergo the evaluation in October 1999 and CPS again found another angle to make me have another evaluation without a court order and my attorney, Grace Kilchenstein, refused to contest it. From 1998 to 2003 I was told to sign court stipulations under threats by the DSS attorney and was never told the right to never sign anything. They repeatedly used my children and the fact I didn't have support as a threat to sign to get reunification of my children. So by the winter of 2000, CPS now stated that I had to comply to another evaluation due to their 15 month rule of termination my rights, covering up their tracks. I had already given them an evaluation from the Division of Vocational Rehabilitation that was a psychological evaluation and at the time I applied for Social Security/SSI for the trauma of losing my 3 children. I also gave CPS an evaluation from the Social Security psychologist. They paid for another psychologist and got the favorable report they wanted to say my rights should be terminated and her evaluation is what made my Social Security case win. So in 2001, I got SSI and I felt so violated by CPS, the repeated unconstitutional psychological evaluations that were not court ordered or done with a guilty verdict by any judge, that I paid $300 for a multi-cultural psychological evaluation with my back SSI settlement money, and got an African-American doctor, Mary Taylor-Ennis from the Institute for Life Enrichment at Good Samaritian Hospital, (I never had any Black doctor evaluate me.) who gave me a favorable report. However, CPS and the juvenile court system is so unjust that they only deal with preponderance of evidence which meant they got as many evaluations they could until they got what they wanted and had a paper trail of over 2000 pages of discovery. They pulled up all my past medical records from childhood, all my psychological records before I had Joshua and was homeless and even when I lived in my parents' home growing up as a Jehovah's Witness. This was in violation of the 4th, 5th, and 14th amendment rights in the Constitution and Bill of Rights rather civil case or criminal. The court system and the public defenders have so many cases and are so insensitive that they habitually paper push cases without telling you your rights. There wasn't any manual or any explanation given how the CINA juvenile court system works and there is a CPS manual all workers must obey but it was not given to me. If you go to any place of business or school they have a manual of rules. Joshua had to repeatedly go to ARD meetings and being that he was special needs I had to get a manual of the laws and rights. CPS, the juvenile court with child abuse cases, and the public defenders office will not tell you anything at least that's how it is in the state of Maryland. So after 2001 they put the petition to terminate my rights of Linda and India and petition to keep Joshua in long term foster care, I contested their petition. Then my attorney, Grace Kilchenstein, told me to plea bargain and terminate my rights. I dropped Ms. Kilchenstein off the case, who has been on the case from 1999 to 2002, and I got another public defender court appointed attorney, Susan Kirwan, who was assigned in 2002. I had Joy 9/21/02 and Susan Kirwan told Master Judge Koban without my consent that I had another baby and CPS came after Joy while she was only 3 weeks old just for having other children in the system without due process. Susan Kirwan is just like Grace Kilchenstein, passive and insensitive ignoring my concerns and she wanted me to terminate my rights volunteerily also. I suggested having another updated evaluation paid by the office of public defender because of being married now and my situation changed. I had the evaluation done in the winter of 2003 and Ms. Kirwan talked the psychologist out of being a supportive witness by telling her legal recommendations to plea bargain and terminate my rights. What upset me is that Joshua has been in several foster homes in the 5 yrs. CPS refused to give me phone calls or any reasonable visits to bond with my children. India and Linda was placed in the same foster home and they are in 2003, forcing to adopt and terminate my parental rights of my daughters. The entire thing has devastated me. I have not even gotten decent photos of all 3 children in the entire 5 years like school pictures or photos from Sears. My daughters are so brainwashed. Joshua has been hospitalized several times in the foster care system and on several medications. The boy is wounded and they treat him less than a child of God. My children are just property to the State. My lawyer, Susan Kirwan, did say something right when she told me I could have abandoned the entire case and left the state, but I kept in contact with CPS and my children. My lawyer said I stayed on the same apartment management property for 12 years which should show how stable I am. I had repeatedly asked for CPS or DSS to provide documentation of what their requirements are for housing for reunification. The CPS worker told me I had to relocate without putting anything in writing. It's too costly to get a 3 -4 bedroom home without proper documentation for HUD and where I am moving to rather in Maryland or out of state. CPS has played games with the entire case. They have contacted my mother who is Jehovah's Witness and very unstable enough for them to use her as a pond. My family disowned me since 18 years old and has never been a stable support to Joshua or my other children. Then all of the sudden in 2003 my family have more rights than I do. The entire thing stressed me out to the point I had severe chest pains. I contacted the governor, the Maryland Dept. of Human Resources (DHR), and the director of the Baltimore City Social Services. They all coward out saying that since the case is in the juvenile court they can not intervene. I told all of them and my attorney that they could get the media involved. I have been concerned that Joshua may have been hurt in the foster care system and they are covering up. The devil doesn't want me to lay eyes on my child especially since I got the Holy Ghost now to discern the spirit of my child. All they are doing is drugging up the child without dealing with his spirit. The boy need Jesus and need to be in a regular church home fellowship. It is my strong hope that Joshua writes a book or tells his story and sue the crap out the system and sue the state of Maryland when he turns 18 years old. That is only 6 years from now! They are taking advantage of him because he is a minor. I pray daily and dream about all 3 of my children.

Everyday I see Joy, I praise the Lord because I thank God they didn't take her too. It is hard to live in the neighborhood and go to church where people know your business and with insensitivity, constantly asking why the children are not home and for 5 years they refused to be a support to get the children back. The worse people to be around, is church folk! They can be cold than the world. I had to go through 5 years without spending holidays, and birthdays with my children. While I was at United Baptist Church dealing with my children being taken, I suffered from so much rejection in the church it was ridiculous. Joshua would tell me before he was taken by CPS in 1998 how members would treat him, and I never paid it any attention because I said he was just a boy. One time Joshua walked to give his life to Christ and they rejected him. My spiritual mom taught Joshua about Jesus and I constantly had videos and music tapes about the Lord and Bible characters that he knew for himself that he wanted to have Jesus in his heart. After United rejected Joshua I felt so bad that I allowed him to go to fellowship which another church that would come every Saturday to pick him up. The boy wanted to be baptized and they said no. He cried and cried that day. Then they allowed other children his age to give their lives to Christ and I was furious. Had they laid hands on Joshua and prayed over him, I believe none of the stuff with CPS would have happened. That is one thing I give to First Apostolic, they lay hands on people and have ministers at alter call rebuking the devil and leading people to be baptized in the Holy Ghost and in the name of Jesus. I think that denominations or religious traditions are not of God and they keep the people in bondage. It's all about relationship with Jesus. There were people in United that had the baptism of the Holy Ghost and Pastor Solomon shut them up. I am so glad God took me out of there. It was a mess. I remember when I first got saved and was in a very abusive relationship, the first lady was having women's workshops, and she did an enactment imitating my relationship, back then I didn't know I was being mocked and made a fool of. I remember crying in her arms in front of everybody because I was saved but being abused at home. The first lady gave me her phone number, I called her, and she gave me fleshly advice to keep my lights on in the house. Oh, come on! Jesus is the light of the world and he lives in me, so what the woman should have done was stir up the gifts and the Holy Ghost in me for comfort, but even the first lady was not rightfully equipped. She should have then made sure I got the baptism of the Holy Ghost. Both Pastor Solomon and his wife speak in tongues but they don't offer that at the alter for people to receive the Holy Ghost like alter call at First Apostolic. I have seen preachers on TBN cable TV that were Baptist freely speak in tongues and make sure people get the baptism of the Holy Ghost. Jesus spoke and the demons listened. When Jesus healed, people did not feel the same way when they left. Something was wrong with the Holy Ghost Sister Solomon had then but now I am mature and know better. Don't get me wrong, Pastor Solomon is an excellent preacher and can tear the house down but he stinks at pasturing especially with what my family needed and he has way too many clicks and clones for me. I have given him and the first lady gifts because God charged me to and I got talked down to for that by the first lady. One night during Bible Study, I was at the alter, which is what Hannah in the Bible did and the priest accused her of being drunk, and Pastor again accused me of getting attention not discerning that I was in need of help and he frankly didn't care. They walked on me and over me while I was at the alter. Then Sister Solomon got in my face and it was all I could do to hit her in her face. The deaconess was there and of course Pastor Solomon ran out. I went off because she said I was giving her husband gifts and running around the church out of decency and order. The pastor and the first lady should have taken me in the office, but no, they were both getting their rocks off on me. It took the minister of music and another minister to calm me down and say it was not worth it. What hurt was not just my pain but the fact they never reached out to help me or my children while in foster care. The truth didn't come out until Joshua was gone. My girlfriend took her children to United and they treated her and the children like a disease, she witnessed it for herself how United and Pastor Solomon is and said not to go to that church. The only time Pastor Solomon would act like he said some sense was when they had noon day service and I loved that because he would have guess speakers preach and it wasn't anybody he was trying to impress and he would preach until the presence of the Lord would come. One Sunday Pastor Solomon preached about Joshua and the Jericho walls so good that I mailed Joshua a copy of it to encourage him in foster care. I mean Pastor pulled some strongholds down that day! I got baptized there in 1993 and they made me feel so bad there that I got baptized again while my children were gone. If I praised the Lord I was walked over, told to sit down, talked about to my face, and even laughed at just like Joshua told me. Then if that wasn't bad enough Pastor Solomon repeatedly, said in the pulpit that I was trying to get attention whenever I praised the Lord. The church treated me like I had seven demons in me but now I know they didn't have no Holy Ghost or the anointing to encourage me. Being there was nothing like at First Apostolic where I got baptized in the Holy Ghost in 2000. They are building a new sanctuary in 2003 but every time I past

United I get bad feelings and despite invitations to come back I say hell no, I am never going back to be a member and be treated less than a sister in Christ. At the first lady's workshop teaching information from her book her got published, she had me on the floor by telling me to lie down and then she had over 5 women by force push me on the floor. She said I was exposed but what she did was so ghetto and out of retaliation. I told my spiritual mom about what Sister Solomon did at the workshop and she said it was ghetto and she wish she was there to beat her tail down. I have yet to heal from that now. Now I am very careful who I trust in the sanctuary. I can bump into somebody from United Baptist church and they will say stupid insulting stuff like, "You can't have another baby! Is this your 10th child?!" This is the devil's way of putting shame on me to the point I don't want to talk or show my face but the devil's a liar! What I went through at United was a test and the devil's way of making feel that if the saints and a pastor rejects me that I was not worthy of anything from God especially dealing with the torment of having my children taken from me. I am covered by the blood of Jesus and His mercy endures forever. I have a termination of parental rights hearing for Linda and India for July 2, 2003 and I have a contesting hearing for Joshua on 6/25/03. Social Services want Joshua in long term foster care because the state gets bounties under the CAPTA laws President Clinton made. They care less about the "best interest of the children", it's all about money. I' m believing God for the miraculous that my son will not be growing up as a teenager in the system. The prayers of the righteous will prevail and no weapon form against me and my family shall prosper. I just don't believe my living and prayers were in vain these 5 years from 1998-2003. Well that's all I want to discuss about the child custody thing. There is somebody out there going through worse than I did with CPS and tests/trials and they need to know just how faithful God is. Look at it this way. I could have been in jail those 5 years, in a mental institution for life, lost my home, killed somebody, on drugs and alcohol, but God made sure his spirit was deposited in me for eternal joy and comfort that the world didn't give and the world can't take away. I serve an awesome God. There is absolutely nothing too hard for God.

This year my parents are divorcing after over 30 years of marriage. The thing has devastated both me and my sister. My mother left my father for an ex-boyfriend who was a high school sweet heart of hers. Coming to find out my mother never let the man go and they had some unfinished business. My grandmother broke my mother and this ex-boyfriend up and my parents got together. My father claims that he never loved my mother because she chased him. To hear the both of them backstab each other this year about the past putting both me and my sister in the middle stressed me out. My mother moved out, got her own place in a fancy apartment high rise complex and kept associating with her ex-boyfriend to the point she almost got excommunicated from the Jehovah's Witness faith. Now it was hard for me to be a support to my mother because I got excommunicated at 18 and was homeless with just the clothes on my back yet my mother wanted me to comfort her. Then my father tells me how he was molested as a child which affected the marriage. I really wanted to flip out from that because I was also molested as a child. My mother was the one that was there when I went to the court house to get married but she would not stay as our witness and she got two strangers to be our witnesses. My husband's friend didn't show up for our witness. That was so embarrassing to have my mother show up and not stay. Then my father wanted me to testify in divorce court against my mother. To tell the truth I wanted to but my husband and spiritual mother told me to honor both parents and stay out of it. The divorce has made me feel like the question to the years of rejection was finally answered. I knew I was unplanned and unwanted but didn't know why. My father never was in love with my mother and still isn't. They just went through the motions for 30 plus years. My sister is really hurt and torn in the middle. My father called me to find out if I have been talking to Endeara, my sister, about getting out Jehovah's Witness. I told him that we talk very brief about her job, my sister going to college, how the divorce is affecting her, and we never talk about religion. In the middle of all of that mess, my father thinks I am going to influence a 21 year old woman to come out a cult. I told him I have my own issues to deal with and he left it at that. To my family I am dead and they still are waiting for me to come back to Jehovah's Witnesses because they honestly believe I will be destroyed at Armageddon by God and that what happened with my 3 children is a punishment and result of not being in the cult or "truth". So when my aunt Linda, my mother's sister, after years of excommunicating me and my children/family, contacted me, I got a lot of pressure from her and her mind still thinks I am 18 years old and back as if I died. She visited my children with my mother for the Child Protective Service visit and flip out on me because I was deeply wounded for not being there. I felt I had more rights then they did to see Joshua. I told my mother and aunt that at least my family could have called Joshua, written him, sent him cards, or something before he was taken and he was in foster care. To all of the sudden tell me flat out they didn't care how I felt and they just wanted to see my children, was a slap in the face. I cried for hours. Yet I had to be a support to my parents for the divorce. Divorce is painful no matter how old the children are. Being married now makes me appreciate how my life changed. I want my entire family saved and true Christians out of Jehovah's Witness. They all need the Holy Ghost. There is too much bondage in the family and all I can do is show them show Christ gives unconditionally love and joy. Here's a poem I wrote, I hope it will encourage:

STILL HOLDING ON!
BY CRYSTAL DIXON

Pressure rising, time flying by
Life's wind blows
Yet, I'm still holding on!
Sometimes confused but focused on Christ
Take baby steps if I have to
While I put my complete trust in Jehovah
My God that heals and equips me in victory.
God is a way out of no way, my shelter I numerous storms.
God is the gentle touch from heaven yet strong enough to conquer all of my enemies.
When Christ died on Calvary, I see his unconditional loving arms open wide just for me.
That all by itself gives me courage to keep holding on!

JESUS + YOU = VICTORY! – PART 2

Dr. Maya Angelou is my all time favorite writers and one of my favorite poems of hers is "Still I Rise". I encourage you to read this poem when you need a pick me up to lift up your spirit. Then after you have meditated on this poem, put yourself in every syllable and phrase and know for a fact that you too will rise above your situation and meet your dreams.

With Jesus at your side day by day, you have the blessed assurance that your faith walk is victorious. Jesus invites you and I to: "Come to me, all you who are weary and burdened, and I will give you rest. Take my yoke upon you and learn from me, for I am gentle and humble in heart, and you will find rest for your souls. For my yoke is easy and my burden is light." (Matthew 11:28-30) What man do you know is like Jesus, compassionate, gentle, humble in heart, self-sacrificing, and he would tell you something like this and mean it?! If you can't think of anyone or are in a relationship that's opposite of Jesus -get out of it. Jesus knows you inside and out for he made you knowing what makes you tick. (Psalms 100:1-5, Psalms 139:13-16) Today the men of the world miss the mark and they are not even whole in Jesus or even have a relationship with God, but they will try to control, manipulate, and play boyish games from woman to woman because YOU let them do it. Realize that God sincerely loves you and keeps his promises. So when God says he will provide and take care of you, he will. When God says he will never leave you or forsake you, he won't. (Hebrews 13:5-6) There are too many desperate, low self esteem females, young and old that actually believe college education, big time jobs, belonging to a club or even going to church will trap themselves a mate or a man-NOT. What real, god fearing, wise, man would want to be your trap unless they are just as desperate and not whole as you are?! If you put God first in EVERYTHING you do, a REAL man will come your way for your not to search, degrade, manipulate, and do God's job for you. The Bible says that whatever you ask God by faith it will be given to you. (Matthew 7:7-12) If God's not in your life or your decisions, Satan will definitely make sure you "sleep with the enemy"! You'll get the tall, dark, and handsome man but deceptiveness, sexually uncleanness, financial bondage, insecurity, and every other stronghold that's the opposite of what you really need than your wants. Paul says in the Bible that your body is the temple of the Holy Spirit, so in other words, your body isn't yours to mistreat with just any old thing. (1 Corinthians 6:19, 20)

Since your body is the temple of the Holy Spirit, make sure before you even think of having somebody else in your life, you cultivate the fruit of the Holy Spirit which is the character and mind of God. (Galatians5:22-26) A woman if she wants a man should desire a husband and not a lover, or boyfriend. She should prepare herself for marriage during her singleness and use Proverbs 31: 10-31 as her guide. Really if God's will isn't for her to marry, yes I said God's will, because marriage is a ministry and sacred to God, it's OK to remain single instead of getting married to get your rocks off in lust for the flesh. Paul stated in 1 Corinthians 7:29-35 that singleness is even better than marriage because marriage restricts ministry freedom and extra devotional time to God's work. So I suggest you be free in Christ and remember that Jesus + You = Victory!

MY TEARS JUST WOULDN'T COME
BY CRYSTAL DIXON

Molested at 4 or 5 years old kept a secret.

Disowned by family and parents at 18 for religion.

Homeless on the streets, not a whore on the corner but a desperate survivor in strangers' homes.

Yet, my tears just wouldn't come…

Raped by an African stranger when my monthly visitor came.

He told me God would bless be after he took what was not his.

My mother betrayed me and for that I was never the same.

Never tried drugs or was completely lost in the world.

Just wanted to be loved, respected, valued, but I was dead to the world.

My tears just wouldn't come…

I met my son's father, 6 years older than I.

I took a lot of abuse from him out of fear.

Refusing to go to my parents, a shelter, the House of Ruth was my home while pregnant with my son, Joshua.

God blessed me with my very first home.

I still went from one bad relationship to another for many years.

Yet, my tears just wouldn't come…

Fought cancer in my body, meet death at my door.

Now I had two children, Joshua and India, by two different fathers, Joshua was disabled and special needs and India just wouldn't talk.

Then my heart was broken when Joshua and India was taken from me in 1998 on Joshua's birthday which started a 5 year legal battle.

I had another daughter, Linda Ann, in 1999 and she was taken because of my other two children was in foster care. They were taken just because I lacked support systems and without criminal charges pressed.

Joshua has been in several foster homes and my daughters were put in the same foster home.
Daily I dreamed of my children coming home and daily my heart hurt for my children as if I was the walking dead.
My tears just wouldn't come…

One day it hit me that Jesus has been there the entire time.
He sent his angels around my life.
He never gave up on me even when I did.
God's strength kept me together all along.
Then I realized my tears were inside the whole time but I had to survive.
Only the strong survive, right?
My tears did come sometimes on my face now and then, but I thought they were invalid to myself and others.
Dead people don't cry, they just exist.
Jesus gave me his Holy Spirit to comfort me to wrap his arms around.
Something on the inside just flowed like water in the river.
I began to cry not tears of hurt and pain, but relief.
Tears of joy to be love by God.
Tears knowing that I am God's child.
Tears knowing that I am more than a conqueror.
God showed me from then on that every tear of mine he held and treasured even when they weren't seen by the naked eye.
The tears came, and kept going on and on…
From that moment on I dedicated my life wholeheartedly worshipping God doing His will.
Now my life has inner peace, contentment, and unending joy. God has wiped my tears and now I am resurrected by His grace.

BATTER'S UP!

BY CRYSTAL DIXON

As children of God living in a dying, immoral world we know for without a shadow of a doubt that these are definitely the "last days".

(Matthew 24) Yes, "the whole world is under the control of the evil one"(1 John 5:19), but "greater is the one who is in you than the one who is in the world". (1 John 4:4-6) Victims of domestic violence, sexual assault, and child abuse have to know that even though Satan used a person to attempt to destroy their purpose and destiny, God's got the world in his hand and will not let them slip through his fingers!

Physical abuse is very painful and even traumatic, but the emotional effects are worse because people can't label or see the seriousness of emotional pain. Yet Jesus Christ died and sacrificed his life for you and I before we came into existence with unconditional love outweighing any abuse. For by his wounds we are healed. (Isaiah 53:5) Never take your circumstances or the abuse personal as an attack on you as if you are less than God's child just because somebody tells you so. The Bible shows at Ephesians 6:10-12 that we are battling against the dark world and spiritual forces of evil in the heavenly realms and not flesh and blood. So be encouraged and use discernment to never go back into an abusive situation again because Christ loves you.

Take one day at a time and one step at a time like a baby. Look at yourself as being on a baseball field playing the game. You are at home plate with your bat but you can only take one base at a time or one trial at a time. Satan is the pitcher, throwing everything he can at you, and you don't know what kind of ball will come your way. Satan says, "Yeah, I'll throw suicide her way. Maybe I can take her self esteem away too. Hold up, I know what, I'll try to get her like I tried to do Job and see if I can get her to curse God." Yes, you may not know the exact tactic Satan will use until he actually throws it, but that's why you have the Bible as your sword or bat. (Hebrews 4:12-13) Satan is so stupid trying to make you loose or get you out of the game that he forgets that there's a major possibility of YOU hitting a major HOMERUN. Even if you get to the next base, that's one mark you weren't on before and one more step to your victory, defeating the devil. When you hit the ball and go to the next base you don't skip, hop, jump, or procrastinate, you RUN and slide on the base if the devil tries to throw the ball and attempts to get you out. You have to look at your situation as if you have already won the game and just giving God glory and worship. God definitely deserves all of your praise despite the bruises on your body or the emotional scars you may have because he gave you mercy and grace with breath in your lungs to tell Satan that he's given you another chance.

So look up to God! The Holy Spirit lives in you and so does God and where the Lord's spirit is there's liberty and freedom. (2 Corinthians 3:17-18) God sees you as a treasure in jars of clay, valuable, for this life is temporary and so are your circumstances – you may be "hard pressed on every side, but not crushed". (2 Corinthians 4:6-18) Always remember that God definitely hears your cries. (Psalms 116)

WOMAN, YOU ARE AWESOME… LET GOD USE YOU! – A PRAYER FOR WOMEN BEFORE THE LORD

BY CRYSTAL DIXON

Father, I come boldly to your throne of grace in behalf of myself and the African American woman. You know everything before I say it, my heart, my mind, my soul, and spirit. You are all powerful, and mighty. For when you speak a word it is so, just like when you spoke light into existence in the beginning of the creation of the earth. You mean what you say! Lord, you created man and woman in your own image separate from the animals with your love, power, wisdom, mercy, and grace. As women we have to use the fullness of every characteristic of YOU inside of us. You put your own breath into Adam, Hallelujah. Out of a rib from Adam came a woman, so we are not junk! Every child birthed comes from a woman, every seed of destiny springs forth from the womb, and that alone makes the woman awesome.

Jesus, you are Lord, risen from the dead and put your resurrection power in us daily. You value the woman and treasured women when you were on the earth. You are the same yesterday, today, and forever. Lord, I lift up women that have been molested and child abused, women that have been prostitutes be it on the streets or not, women that had abortions killing your promised seeds, women that are on drugs and substance abusers to seek love, and women that just haven't found you to be their Lord and savior. Lord, you used Rahab in the Bible to hide the spies despite her being a prostitute and because of her faith not only her family was saved but you, Jesus, came from her family line. (Joshua Chapter 2, Hebrews 11:30,31) Oh, yeah, remember how you used the prophetess Deborah as judge over your people and how she stated that the Lord will hand Sisera over to a woman. She was 100% right because you use Jael to pick up a tent peg and hammer and drive the peg into Sisera's head while he was asleep, exhausted. (Judges 4) Remember Lord the faith of the Canaanite woman you actually called a dog because she wasn't of God's people, stopping you to heal her daughter suffering from demon-possession. She told you, Lord: "Yes, Lord, but even the dogs eat the crumbs that fall from their masters' table." You had to stop and bless her out of compassion. Then if that's not enough, Lord, how many times did you tell your disciples (men at that) how you would die and rise up out of the grave and their faith didn't believe your words, yet a woman, Mary Magdelene, saw your resurrected body at the entrance of your empty tomb, and all you had to say was "Mary" in such a way only she could know it was you. In return, Mary cried out in Aramaic, "Rabboni!" (which means Teacher) and went to the disciples, your posse and men that walked and talked with you all during your ministry on earth, and they didn't believe her until you showed up face to face. Women are definitely your instrument and need to stop being mistreated, misunderstood, but used for your glory and honor just like in times of old. Women are something to be reckoned with and treasured!

Lord, I pray that women today catch on fire for you and get into your presence seeking your face. For can't nobody do a woman like you, Jesus, can't nobody do use like you, Lord! For just like when Moses had so much of your glory on his face that the Israelites couldn't look directly into Moses' face, so I pray every woman have the Holy Spirit so evident in their lives that people will see God. (2 Corinthians 3:7-18) Just like Stephen was seized and persecuted, you anointed him so good that as "all who were sitting in the Sanhedrin looked intently at

Stephen, they say that his face was like the face of an angel." (Acts 6:15) You are Jehovah, the Great I AM, you are righteous, and full of love, so extend your love to all of your chosen people, women of God. Let them know that your love is in them completely despite the lies Satan the devil tells them. Fill their hearts and minds with peace and make them whole, complete in YOU.

This is your humble servant's prayer for your holy people; and I believe it won't come back unfulfilled, null and void, because I am standing on your Word and promises and just for who you are as GOD.

Amen.
Amen.
Amen.

WITHOUT YOUR TRUE LOVE...
BY CRYSTAL DIXON

Ever increasing, always enduring, the presence of our love.
Gentle, compassionate, understanding eyes I see
Clearly day by day protecting over me.
Ignorance try to prevail asking how you came to be.
Yet it just doesn't matter because finally I'm free.
Free to be caught up in your loving arms; free to
Vision fulfilling every godly destiny.

You have always been there patiently waiting for me
To make up my mind traveling life's bumpy road.
Your love letters to me and spirit kept me together all these years.
Through adolescence, young adulthood, rearing children, you've watched me grow up from a distance but never stopped offering your open arms to come running back to.

When I lost my soul mate to another, Death himself almost snatched me up and I didn't mind him knocking on the door.
You refused to allow me to give up and offered a lifetime vow; how could I dare say no.
From that moment on I have hope, peace, unspeakable joy, and more than a reason to exist and live.
I deeply thank you with ALL of my heart despite the reality of having a small piece of it still wounded and loving the soul mate I lost.

Every time we make love I keep on believing and receiving all of the visions and dreams our spirits connecting express.
The prosperity, tranquility, wholeness, and all the never-ending possibilities.
For not once has there ever been a promise you've broken to me.
Distant love, not so.
Ending love, never, never let go.
Inhale, exhale every breath, every second is full of thanksgiving.
What would I be without your true love…

LIFE'S A REAL ROLLERCOASTER…

BY CRYSTAL DIXON

Get on at your own risk. Only people this tall can get on.
Looking up at the hills, twists and turns fear creeps in.
There's a long line to get on but I'm 21+ and grown to handle it.
Mature to young in years' screams almost echo the entire park.
I get on alone without friends or relatives with a total stranger at my side held by a metal bar.
Skeek, skeek, skeek, the tracks sound as the carriage slowly climbs up the hill.
As I go way up in the air with my guts feeling as if they're outside, I lift up my hands and scream like ten other people on the ride and the intensity of the thrill subside.

There's some on the ride that never scream or even sweat as the ride takes hoops, goes upside down, and goes wild.

Life is a rollercoaster.
You'll have your ups and downs, twists, and turns.
Sometimes you'll think you're big and bad to handle life's challenges alone knowing the risks you have or choose to take.
Watch out, once you're strapped down and it's just you, with the road in life you've chosen, and God, you have to hang on in there!
The thing I like about life with God is that when you go through trials and tests you can always look up and reach down from within with Holy Ghost praise, lifting up holy hands and the spirit of fear flees. Hallelujah!
Just like a rollercoaster in a park, you can choose which ride to get on, which risk on each you want to ignore, and how well you're going to handle the thrill. Are you going to react like others before or after you?

Life's rollercoaster, trials, tribulations give us testimonies to make us overcomers. Notice that many people get the nerve to even get right back on the ride after the screams, and the guts on the floor because they made it through the ride. Believe you me, Satan will challenge you with some of the same hills, twists, and turns but you can overcome conquering every stupid challenge from hell victoriously.

My deepest prayer is for people to boldly walk with Jesus and realize we are more than conquerors.

RAISING A SPECIAL NEEDS CHILD
(written in 1997 and dedicated to Joshua Sweeney, my son)
BY CRYSTAL DIXON

I am a 27-year-old woman, a mother of two young children, and wonder how in the world I make it with struggling to raise a 6-year-old son with severe emotional disorders. By the grace and guidance of God I find that all things are possible and can be done. My son gives me intense strength and no matter what, I love him unconditionally. He isn't special needs because of the label society stamped him with, on the contrary, he's special because of the destiny and purpose God has in store for him.

My son really saved my life when conceived. If it weren't for his existence and birth, I believe I would still be homeless, a battered woman, and possibly dead. My son had been disabled since 10 months old with developmental delays, physical setbacks, chronic ear infections resulting in PE tubes, and once he turned 3 years old his behavior became severe. Joshua has seen too much as a little boy. He has been rejected by daycare centers, mistreated in churches, observed abusive men in my life, hasn't seen any decent family support systems in his life, and now that he is 6 years old he battles so much inner anger it's depressing for a mother to watch. Sometimes I blame myself for everything, wishing I could take everything away but I can't. It's very difficult to raise him because he hits me out in public, damages property in my home, and now he will not do any school work. I hate to see his anger put him in prison when he gets older or set him back. As a believer in Christ, I firmly believe Joshua is an overcomer and just going through a stage. How do I continue to help find out what's in his mind and heart to get to the root of the problem? Psychologist, hospitals, schools, and special programs just don't cut it any longer because they only confuse everything and make a young black child hopeless being pushed through the system. What would you do if you were me?

Joshua now has a sister, India, to share when before everything was just him. Financially, emotionally, and now health wise I can't nurture him like he was at 3 years old because my daughter is also trying to follow her brother's footsteps with developmental delays. It's hard to find employment or childcare because I don't trust society with my children, not just because of their setbacks but because they are all I have. I have attended college sacrificing my son for education and I regret it down to this day. So I try to make a life at home with my children the best I can, never giving up on my goals. I find out that staying focused in life, not letting society's standards control you, and remaining patient within yourself is vital raising a special needs child. My family faced complete persecution from family and friends, poverty, and yet we are content in life with God first in our lives. Social workers and agencies have tried to repeatedly label me an unfit mother because I manage to survive on my own in a manner society believes is unreal by me having no support systems as a single parent. My children will travel all over the world anywhere they want to go, have a college education, and make a concrete mark on the world.

One day when Joshua has his own children I know he will appreciate the sacrifices made, the spankings, the hours helping him with his homework while he hit his mother, the protective ways I screened his friends and unnecessary folk in his life, and then he will thank me praising God. Joshua is a leader not a follower. It's just that right now he has to be molded, cultivated, and trained in the proper way to go which may take years, TLC, in a special way different from other children his age. Joshua will be successful. One should never underestimate the great things God can and will do with a little child!

THROUGH CRYSTAL'S EYES – PART 3

It is June 7, 2003 and I am missing my 3 children like crazy. Joshua's 12th birthday is on June 19, 2003 and I am not allowed to see him because of his psychologist in foster care recommends blocking visits. The fact of the matter is there has never been a court order by a judge saying I am guilty of anything and the psychologist never had a court order for the recommendation. The psychologist has blocked visits with Joshua since 1999 without any court appointed attorney contesting it to protect my rights to see Joshua. I got the following letter from MENTOR, which is the psychological group CPS paid by contract to care for Joshua without a court order or giving me any chance to contest medical care by MENTOR:

The Mentor Network
Mentor Maryland
7127 Ambassador Road
Baltimore, Maryland 21244
phone 410-944-5055 1-800-846-0071 fax 410-944-5581
www.thementornetwork.com

May 23, 2003

Dear Ms. Dixon,

We have had several discussions about visitation between you and Joshua. I am writing to clearly state our position about the visitation.

Joshua is a Severely Emotionally Disturbed child. He has a history of explosive and aggressive behavior which has led to several psychiatric hospitalizations. When the explosive episodes occur, Joshua has broken windows, assaulted and bitten others, and been extremely verbally aggressive. These episodes often occur without warning and can last for long periods of time. Police intervention has been necessary to help subdue Joshua on the last 2 occassions.

Joshua has not seen you for several years. Furthermore, he has been very stable in his present home. He has developed a strong relationship with his current foster parents. We are concerned that he would react very strongly to a visit with you. If he became explosive and destructive after a visit with you, he would run the risk of losing this placement. There are no others homes within our program. If he loses this placement, he would have to be placed in a program outside of Mentor.

I am sure that you would want Joshua to maintain the stability that he has experienced recently. It is our judgement that we cannot run the risk of disrupting the current placement. Therefore, we are recommending that Joshua not have visits with you.

This letter will be sent to Ms. Animashaun and Ms. Kirwan and will represent our position at the court hearing on June 25. If you have any questions, you may call any one of us at 410-944-5055.

Sincerely,

Braxton Andrews, LCSW-C Kim Adgerson, LGSW Donna Dryer, MD

CC Susan Kirwan Esq
Ms. Rita Animashaun

This letter got me so depressed because who wants to hear negative things about their first born son and can't be there to comfort or help him. Here's a letter I got from a coalition in support of my CPS case:

New Justice System Coalition for the Reform of Child Abuse Enforcement Laws.

NJS Coalition

Suite 1, 252 Main Street West

Hamilton, Ontario.

L8P1J6

Canada

Date June 4, 2003

Dear Crystal:

Here are the laws that will stop the action from taking place. You will have to insert the fine detail on this motion and file it yourself or have your attorney file it. This should put you on the road to your children. God bless

This area is for the name of the court

jurisdiction of case. All of this can be

Found at the top of your court records.

Case # goes here

Crystal Yvonne Dixon

The name of the department here: Plaintiff

VS

Your name here: Defendant

Others name if any: Defendant

List each child's name and social security# with date of birth;   Defendant

example Child 1, 000-00-0000, 0/00/00   Defendant

Child 2, 000-00-000, 0/00/00   Defendant

Motion to Strike Plaintiffs brief under color of the law of this land.

Now comes the plaintiff Crystal——and for her motion does state and allege that the department has acted under color of the law of this land. That the department has suppressed material information clearly favorable to the named defendants named above. That all reasonable services have not been provided to the child in this case. That the evidence presented does not show clear and convincing grounds of termination as outlined in state and federal laws of this land. The following is respectfully presented as follows:

1. Constitutional Law is the noted law of this land. Constitutional law is quoted 746 head note (14) "Due process is flexible and calls for such procedural protections as the particular situation demands" No lead way has been given to the fact this family suffers from disabilities that could effect their ability to comply with the demands of the department. As quoted in State VS Kelly, 216 kan. 311, 531P. 2nd 60.

2. It was established in Brady VS Maryland, 373 US. 83, 10 L.ED 2nd 215, 835 Ct 1194; "Withholding and suppressing material information clearly favorable to the defendant is impeachable"

3. It has been a well know fact to every parent that Foster care is a commitment of children to a governmental system. That this deprives parents and children to restrictions of all basic freedoms. Addington VS Texas, 4411US, 418, 425 (1979) does state" That commitment for any purpose constitutes a significant depravation of liberty that requires Due Process protection." In O'connor VS Donaldson, 422US. 563, 574 (1975) That a state must have a Constitutionally adequate purpose for confinement.

4. The children of our land are guaranteed full protection of the law under our Constitution. This is up held in Article 14 section and Article 4 section 4. When the department fails to provide reasonable services to comply with the federal requirements of the US they are withholding the child's right to Due process of the law.

5. Privacy regulations were created as a result to the Health Insurance Portability and Accountability Act of 1996. When the department force a parent to sign releases in order to receive services they are holding children for ransom for services. Placing all family members in double jeopardy in order to be in compliance with a lower court order.

6. All mental and physical disorders are to be proven by a higher degree of standard than preponderance of evidence. Leland Vs Oregon, 343 US. 790, 799 (1952). When the department uses preponderance of evidence in a child case to judge a parent it forces the court to be put in the position of jeopardy on constitutional issues. That will lead the court in to an abuse of discretion under the American with disability Act.

7. In Fink VS Neil 328 Ark. 646, 945 S.W. 2nd 9116 (1997) It was established that" when a series of errors are prejudicially entered

as fact the case has entered the realm of harassment. Which leaves the department and the court in jeopardy of prosecution.

The above named defendant prays the court will respectfully hear the above named objections of law and strike the termination of rights in this case. Under lack of services offered to parents and under constitutional objections put forth.

Allowing the attorney of record the time to have such objections reviewed by the Attorney General of this state.

Respectfully submitted

We offer this consultation based upon your request for help from the NJS Coalition. We hope that any further assistance that you may need will not be hesitated upon in your asking. This coalition has been based in Canada with offices in the U.S. Your main contact with the coalition will be Tim Shepherd. All correspondence via U.S. Postal Service shall be handled by our Home office in Ontario Canada. Please read and understand the disclaimer of liability attached at the bottom of this letter.

Sincerely,

Tim Shepherd

Ceo

Disclaimer of Services

The services provided within these communications are not to be considered professional legal advice. Advice of an advocate of this organization is given freely and by request of the individual provided for. At no time shall NJS or any of its affiliates be proclaimed as lawyers. NJS and its affiliates will be held harmless by any and all client/victims and affiliated personnel.

I thought this was a powerful tool to fight my case especially after getting the letter from MENTOR blocking visits without a court order. I have a contesting hearing for all 3 of my children (Joshua, India, and Linda) on 6/25/03 and my court appointed attorney is giving me a hard time because she rather me quit and terminate my rights to make it easy on her instead of being effective with the case. I don't believe a word in the letter MENTOR sent, if anything I believe they have done some harm to my son and have tried to cover it up. I sent my attorney the following motion for visitation to fight for my children and she has ignored it out of fear of contesting and fighting for my rights as a court appointed attorney:

MOTION FOR MORE FREQUENT AND MEANINGFUL VISITATION

IN RE: Joshua Sweeney-Bey, Linda Bey, India Sweeney-Bey
Petition numbers:898170004, 898170005,899224004

IN THE CIRCUIT COURT
BALTIMORE CITY
DIVISION FOR JUVENILE CAUSES

Crystal Dixon, mother of children, moves the court for an order granting more frequent and meaningful visitation and bonding with her children listed above. Specifically, mother requests:

1) Visitation to occur at least 3 times per week and each visit lasting at least 3 hours

2) Visitation to be unsupervised with the stipulation of a specific time for the children to arrive and be picked up to return to the CPS worker.

3) Visitation to be as home visits with the presence of the children's attorney, the mother's attorney, GAL or CASA for the children, audio and video taped for proper documentation to prevent governmental abuse, and the presence of support systems (grandparents, father of children, church support, friends of mother) at each visit. The visit can be arranged at the grandparents' home, during church services for mid week services, at a neutral public place like a park, McDonalds, or places of bonding where the environment is less restrictive with the presence of a court mediator, the children's attorney, and video taping for the court record.

4) Supervised phone calls by 3 way daily to each child. Photos of all 3 childen every 3 months or more for bonding. Downloading of photos on the internet to mother's computer by CPS and foster parents of all 3 children with scanner and technology to bond with all 3 children. Copies of school progress notes and report cards of India and Joshua.

5) Visitation on all children's birthdays and holidays for bonding or either one day after or before their birthdays and holidays. Mother should have a visit to make up for birthdays and holidays for each child.

6) CPS/DSS should provide transportation to all visits and pay for transportation by court order without any excuses and demanding mother to pay for transportation. CPS should be court ordered to pay for cab vouchers to and from each visit to ensure transportation. Kennedy Institute, Baltimore City Infants and Toddlers Program and DSS all have provided cab transportation vouchers without any difficulties before the CINA in 1998.

7) All medical appointments, hospitalizations, and counseling by psychologists should be done with the mother present with the children's attorney, the attorney of the mother, and children's grandparents present. As long as the visit to the above are all court order supervised visits there should not be any problems. My rights were never terminated from 1998 to 2002. DSS has limited guardianship which means my parental rights are still the same.

Support systems of the mother should be able to come with her to all places mentioned above.

STATEMENT OF FACTS

1) CPS never had the visits court ordered so that meant that they arranged the visits based upon their convenience and the foster parents' feelings or schedule.

2) I was never ruled guilty by a judge of abuse or neglect so none of my visits should have been supervised until a judge or a court order after a guilty verdict mandated I needed supervised visits.

3) CPS failed to provide transportation to the visits from 1998 to 2003

4) I completed the CPS contract which was signed without the presence of my court appointed attorney and never contested under duress and under the color of law violating federal constitutional rights and due process. The CPS contract by Ms. Aronda Okojie was completed by May 1999 without any guilty verdict by a judge or a trial hearing. Parenting classes and a psychological evaluation was done by May 1999.

5) Visits were stated on the CPS contract as biweekly however CPS was inconsistent. I should have gotten weekly visits, home visits, visits at least 3 hours long, and should have been treated as innocent until a judge proved me guilty. There wasn't any court appointed attorney to protect my privacy rights, disability rights, constitutional rights, Bill of Rights Amendments in federal laws. and contest CPS allegations.
6) CPS failed to provide alternatives to bonding.

GROUNDS FOR MOTION

1) Frequent and meaningful visitation is in the best interest of the children.

WHEREFORE, Crystal Dixon, prays for an order directing CPS agency to provide frequent and meaningful visitation and that such visitation by court order commence immediately

Respectfully submitted

Crystal Dixon, Mother of Children

I have been very physically sick from the entire 5 year legal battle and missing my children. What I am concerned about is Joshua feeling I abandoned him and don't love him. I feel that Joshua has blamed himself for what happened to his sisters and myself and that is why he is acting out of his pain. I sent the coalition and my attorney the following CPS story as testimony for court and I feel that Joshua is just a way for the state to make money off of him by keeping him in long term foster care against constitutional and due process rights.

Regarding DSS and CPS allegations of 4/2/96 and 6/18/98

1. In 1995, my son Joshua Sweeney-Bey was regularly seen by Susan Parks and Dr. Harrison through Kennedy Krieger Institute behavioral clinic for home visits and clinic appointments.

2. In early 1996 at Dunbar Daycare Center my son Joshua had a tantrum in the snow, fell outside, hit his face and head. He alleged to the daycare director that I hit him when I was trying to do behavior modification techniques I had learned at the Institute.

3. Susan Parks recommended I admit my son voluntarily at Johns Hopkins Hospital for his behavior. He was in the hospital for one week, they did a few tests, he had 20 minute tantrums where 3 or more people had to retrain him, and Johns Hopkins Hospital still released him.

4. I had to admit him again for the same reasons, asked for thorough testing, for him to be on Ritalin or medication.

5. I was under doctor's orders to be on bed rest for a high risk pregnancy, but was charged as unfit and negligent because the doctor, social workers forced me to retrain Joshua alone despite my health and pregnancy.

6. Joshua's doctor, Dr. Fong in Johns Hopkins Hospital unit labeled me "mentally unstable" to care for Joshua because I challenged everything, and asked for more intensed help for Joshua to be in the Children's Guild or a structured care environment.

7. My parents had Joshua for 30 days and this is why the DSS allegation /petition was denied 4/2/96.

8. I went to all scheduled appointments for Joshua, and mental health care at Total Health Care with psychologist, Rosemary Cook.

9. I got Joshua back with DSS charges unsubstantiated and off the central registry. There was an in-house review of the child abuse/neglect record by Sheritta Barr-Stanley and letter dated 5/31/96 stating the in-house review found my case "unsubstantiated" and that I will be expunged from the record and my name will not be entered into the central registry.

10. On 9/17/96 child abuse was reported again by Johns Hopkins Hospital East Baltimore Mental Health Partnership

11. The family resource coordination unit progress not dated 9/17/96 read as follows written by Wanda Bassett, MSW:

After consulting with supervisor, Myra Kul, a call was made to CPS to report physical abuse. Crystal was also contacted by the RS so feedback could be provided regarding the CPS investigation. Crystal explained that she had gotten little sleep during the night due to concerns involving DSS. RS supported Crystal's concerns. RS also inquired if a home visit could be made to explore other concerns involving Joshua an d the phone call to CPS. Shortly, after RS arrived, a BCPO arrived to complete the report by asking Crystal and Joshua questions about the incident.

Then, Crystal was asked to dress Joshua for a visit to Johns Hopkins Hospital ER for further evaluation by a physician. When evaluated by the physician, Joshua often inconsistent regarding the bruise located on forehead. After Joshua's examination, the physician indicated that the bruise could have been caused by a door knob or someone striking him with an object (Joshua alternated between the two explanations) as indicated by the age of the bruise. The physician intended to reveal this information in his final report.

12. The progress note dated 9/17/96 also stated: Client's mental status as neat, appropriately dressed, appropriate affect, calm mood, appropriate attention, adequate judgement, and clear thought content.

13. The progress note by Wanda Bassett, MSW again dated 10/23/96 stated: RS contacted Mr. Pentzek regarding Joshua's CPS case. He explained that the investigation would be concluded after an interview with Dr. Harrison, Joshua's therapist at Kennedy Kriegar Institute was conducted. He also explained that Crystal seems to be doing "the best she can". Additionally, he would not make a referral to the continuing care unit because already has many service providers involved. Action Plan: RS will contact Mr. Pentzek to follow up on concluding interview with Kelly Harrison.

14. Another progress report was made by Wanda Bassett dated 11/12/96: RS received a message from Crystal regarding an emergency. Thus, RS contacted Crystal involving the crisis. Crystal explained that she was experiencing low mood due to the weekend events. She further explained that she asked her boyfriend to leave the home. She also explained that safety involving herself was a concern. RS inquired if Crystal contacted the police. She reported that she had not, however, an officer advised her to file a restraining order. RS also encouraged Crystal to contact BCPO. Crystal explained that she would do so after talking to her advocate, Patricia Barger of Kennedy Krieger Institute. Joshua seemed to be in good spirits as he watched

Disney movie. He explained that he was ready to attend the family meeting at Kennedy Krieger Institute with his mother.

15. CPS allegations on 6/18/98:

    a. I took Joshua 6/17/98 to see his psychologist, Dr. Kleiner, to update him on Joshua's behavior.

    b. I was unable to schedule regular visits with his doctor due to Joshua going to school 6:30am to sometimes 5 pm on the school bus.

    c. I gave Dr. Kleiner a copy of Joshua's lawyer information for a school bus accident that happened a month earlier, and discussed options for assistance.

    d. On 6/18/998 the day before my son's birthday, Joshua had a 11:30am appointment with Barbara Burns, his new nurse practitioner for the first time for his 7 year old check up. My children never had a doctor or pediatrician.

    e. 3 days before prior to Joshua's check up appointment, Joshua burned India's foot with an iron and I did first aid on India's foot. The children were in the bedroom playing together while I was in the kitchen cooking. The burn was strictly an accident. I don't know exactly how my daughter's foot got burned. I bandaged the foot, put ointment on the foot, and did exactly what I learned from my first aid and CPR course. I called the doctor and was told to wait until Joshua's appointment to bring India in for the foot since the injury was not bad. I called the on call emergency doctor and explained the incident and the injury and was told to wait until that Friday to bring both children in at the same time.

    f. I went to the 6/18/98 clinic appointment with both children for my son's check up thinking I'd be in and out of the clinic. I had to repeatedly warn Joshua about his behavior in the waiting room. Joshua hit a child in the waiting room and I took him to the rest room to discipline him. He fought me in the rest room which caused attention and the doctors and social workers came and took Joshua from me in the back. I should have left hours ago and rescheduled the visit when I noticed we were in the waiting room over 3 hours.

g. Barbara Burns and John Garity, the nurse practitioner and the social worker, didn't know anything about my son's medical history and I was in tears the entire time asking for help. They told me to take India out, I took her out for lunch, came back and they called CPS on me asking me to sign papers. I would not sign any papers and asked for them to give my son medication or hospitalize him for his behavior. I asked them to treat India for her foot and they stated it was fine. They made an appointment for me to come back for a follow up for her foot before they called CPS. There wasn't any photos taken of her foot for child abuse and the police was not called for child abuse.

g. I waited until 6:30/7pm came while they interrogated Joshua and kept me in the waiting room until CPS was contacted behind my back. I talked to the security guard and then found out that they were taking my children from me. They snatched India out my arms. I went senseless from the trauma fighting for my children being taken out my arms. I was handcuffed by police, taken to the ER psychiatric unit, drugged up overnight, and never told where my children were taken. I was not given a chance to appear in any shelter hearing to contest the court because I was detained in the hospital and suffering from the drugs they gave me. CPS and the doctors at Johns Hopkins Hospital falsely charged me with schizophrenia.

16. 1998 I was assigned Aronda Okojie as my CPS worker. My children were place for one month with my parents 8/98 without CPS support to maintain placement and I was not told until I went to court in the Fall of 1998 where my children were. I didn't have any court dates until Fall 1998 before a master judge and I was forced to comply to the CPS service plan and do whatever the

system had me to do without contesting the initial allegations or a fair trial before the judge. I only had one service plan from the fall of 1998 to the summer of 1999 written by Ms. Okojie and one for Joshua's father for the same time frame. The entire 5 years from 1998 to 2003 I didn't get any more service plans or any assistance.

17. I got pregnant with my 3rd child in 1998. I completed the parenting classes and everything on the CPS service plan written by Ms. Okojie which included having me complete a psychological evaluation before 6/99. My public defender didn't contest having any evaluations due or the service plan done until there was a trial and she didn't fight for my constitutional rights or disability rights. I was not told the CINA procedure for the juvenile court, I was not given a CPS manual, and I was pushed through the system by my attorney, CPS, and the DSS attorney to sign all court stipulations under duress to get my children.

18. I was forced to wait until my 3rd child was born despite completing the contract by CPS because my attorney personally felt I should wait and went along with Ms Okojie despite my contesting both of them wanting my children home June 1999. I was forced to have 2 paid off psychological evaluations by CPS until they got the results they wanted to state I have a 10 year mental health record with "personality disorder" and would recommend my parental rights be terminated due to mental illness. CPS made me undergo a 24/7 supervision contract by CPS and my parents when I had my 3rd child at Johns Hopkins Hospital knowing that my parents put my other two children back into the system in 1998 and was not supportive. I lost my 3rd child into the system and CPS took Linda without my attorney contesting anything.

19. I paid for a multi cultural psychological evaluation to be done by a Black doctor and the report was favorable but not enough for the other CPS contracted doctors

20. A sheriff came to my home with a summons for a 6 month review hearing on 10/11/02 after I already had copies. My attorney called

the judge and told her I had a baby and would not be able to come. The judge sent CPS to my home without any written papers to search my home and search my baby. This was done against constitutional rights because my attorney breached client-attorney privacy. All the attorney had to say was she was new to the case and needed more time.

21. I had a psychological evaluation done by the Office of Public Defender arranged in my attorney's office. My attorney wanted me to terminate my rights and give up the case because she stated the odds were against me. I continued to contest. She talked the psychologist after a 5 hour evaluation into plea bargaining me to terminate my rights and to not speak up in my defense. So she wasted my time and hers.

22. CPS have not provided transportation the entire 5 years, disability accommodations the entire 5 years, and they refused to allow me to see Joshua since 1999 due to his psychologist recommendations without any court order or judge ruling.

I have contacted the governor and the policy analyst at DHR to get Joshua out the system. I have contacted the ACLU and I got the following letter:

American Civil Liberties Union Foundation of Maryland
Meadow Mill at Woodberry
3600 Clipper Mill Road Suite 350
Baltimore, Maryland 21211
www.aclu-md.org

June 6, 2003

RE: ACLU File No.: 03B-1425

Dear Ms. Dixon:

We have reviewed your request for legal assistance. As you might be aware, the ACLU is funded by voluntary private donations. Our legal staff is quite small, and most of the cases we accept must be handled by lawyers in private practice who donate their time without charge. As a result, we can offer legal assistance in only a small number of cases each year.

On the basis of the material you supplied, we have concluded the ACLU is unable to assist you in this matter. Please be assured, however, that our decision in no way reflects on the worthiness of your case. We suggest you contact three organizations that provide legal assistance to income-eligible people in a variety of cases to see if they can assist with your complaint. They are: the Baltimore Bar Project (410)539-3112), the Maryland Volunteer Lawyers Service (800-510-0050 or 410-547-6537), and FIP Legal Clinic (800-773-4340). You might also contact the Legal Aid Bureau for your area to determine whether they can represent you. If your case is scheduled to be heard in court, you should contact the Legal Aid office in the area where the case will be heard. Otherwise, you should contact the office nearest your residence. A list of Legal Aid offices in Maryland is enclosed.

You also may want to contact the Maryland Disability Law Center at 1800 N. Charles St. Suite 202, Baltimore, MD 21201 410-727-6352 and the Women's Law Center's Family Law Hotline at 1-800-845-8550. The hotline operates between 9:30 am and 4:30 pm Tuesdays and Thursdays.

We regret we cannot help you further with this matter, and regret the impersonality of this form letter.

Very truly yours

Sonia Kumar
Legal Program Associate

Here's two letters I got from Christopher J. McCabe, Secretary Designee from the Maryland Governor's office:

February 3, 2003

DHR
Maryland Human Services Agency
State of Maryland Department of Human Resources

311 West Saratoga Street
Baltimore, Maryland 21201-3521
Toll Free 800-332-6347 www.dhr.state.md.us

Thank you for your e-mail to Governor Robert L. Ehrlich, Jr, regarding your concern for the well-being of your son, Joshua Sweeney, who currently is in foster care. Governor Ehrlich received your e-mail and asked me to respond to you on his behalf.

It is my understanding that Shirley Brown, Policy Analyst in our Office of Children and Family Services, contacted you to discuss your concerns. Ms. Brown learned that you have not seen Joshua since 1999, the result of a psychiatrist's recommendations. Additionally, you are scheduled to attend a court hearing on February 6, 2003, that will consider termination of parental right, with regard to your daughters, India and Linda Sweeney. You stated goal is the return of all three children. As you may aware, decisions regarding custody are within the purview of the court, which will examine the evidence prior to making its decision. Neither the Governor nor the Department of Human Resources has any jurisdiction or authority to interfere with the judicial process for child custody. Accordingly, it is important that you confer with your attorney regarding the facts related to your case.

Thank you again for writing to Governor Ehrlich. In the future, please do not hesitate to contact me regarding any programs or services administered by the Department of Human Resources.

Sincerely

Christopher J. McCabe
Secretary Designee

cc: Shirley Brown

April 4, 2003

DHR
Maryland Human Services Agency
State of Maryland Department of Human Resources

311 West Saratoga Street
Baltimore, Maryland 21201-3521
Toll Free 800-332-6347 www.dhr.state.md.us

Dear Ms. Dixon:

Thank you for your most recent e-mail to Governor Robert L. Ehrlich Jr., which was in response to the letter dated February 3, 2003, that I wrote you on behalf of the Governor. In my letter, you were informed of the Governor's inability to intervene in the judicial process in matters of child custody. You were advised to consult your attorney regarding an impeding hearing related to the termination of parental rights involving two daughters.

In your e-mail you expressed dissatisfaction with the nature of legal representation you have received in you attempt to regain custody of your children, who are currently in foster care. Of particular concern to you has been the lack of focus on matters related to your son, who is reported to have special needs.

It appears that you have been presented with a number of options for legal representation; therefore, I encourage you once again to explore them fully, including conferring with your attorney. As I had previously written, neither the Governor nor the Department of Human Resources has any jurisdiction or authority to interfere with the judicial process for child custody.

Thank you again for writing to Governor Ehrlich and for sharing your thoughts about the situation involving your children. I hope you can obtain the support that you seek from your attorney.

Sincerely

Christopher J. McCabe

Here's a letter I got for the director's office of the Department of Social Services:

December 17, 199

Department of Social Services
Yvonne Gilchrist, Director
1510 Guilford Avenue
P.O. Box 17259
Baltimore, MD 21203-7259

Writer's number: 410-361-2855

I am in receipt of your letter dated November 24, 1999 regarding your children, Joshua, India, and Linda. I have reviewed with staff your concerns. Baltimore City Department of Social Services is committed to meeting the needs of your children while they are in out-of home-care. One of our critical work decisions is the permanent living arrangements.

Your concerns around the legal issues involving termination of your parental rights would best be addressed through discussions with your appointed attorney. The entire process will later be handled by Juvenile Court.

A new worker, Ms. Rita Animashaun, will be working with your family and will contact you to arrange a monthly visit with your children in January 2000. She will provide bus tokens to assist you with transportation. It is very important that you contact her at (410) 361-4281. If you have other questions and want to reach her supervisor, you may call Mrs. Beverly McDermott at (410)361-4382.

My best wishes to you and your family.

Sincerely

Claudietta Johnson
Assistant Director
Family and Children's Services

Thank God for the Holy Ghost and thank God for the blood of Jesus or else I would have given up a long time ago. Then on 6/7/03 I got the most beautiful letter from a friend of mine that is in prison facing 18 years but I know first hand that God is in his life. I was there when he got shot and had to go to the hospital. He is a walking miracle! In his letter he said, "Failure is never final for those who begin again with Christ!!" This is what gave me a little more wind beneath my wings to get the victory for my family and for Joshua. I was having problems at home with my husband and taking care of a 8 month old infant that is disabled. I needed encouragement to trust the Lord. So, Ronald this one is for you! You inspired me in this book I am writing and in my life, God bless you, man. I love you with the love of Jesus! You are proof that there is life beyond the grave! For you to encourage me in prison the way you did shows just how anointed you really are.

It's June 19, 2003 and I was not allowed even a phone call to bond with my son on his 12th birthday. Here's a letter I sent him through my attorney:

June 19, 2003

Dear Joshua:

It really hurt your father and I to not talk to you on your 12th birthday. I have sent gifts to you from the time they stole you and India in foster care in 1998 on your birthday only for Ms Animashaun to say to you the gifts were not from me. I wanted to be there or call you when you were in the hospital and I wanted to have family counseling with you from 1998 to 2003. What I don't understand is if Dr. Dryer, Ms. Animashaun, and CPS gave your grandmother, my mother, more rights to visit you and take photos with you great aunt and you aunt Endeara, then why in 5 years could they not arrange hospital visits with your grandparents or other family members while the police were called and you were in the hospital. Why didn't they contact your grandmother since she is a nurse to talk to you on the phone and help you heal from what happened. Even now as I am writing this letter which is yours to keep from now until you are an adult and old enough to sue CPS and MENTOR for what they are lying about under the statement, "best interest of the child" because you are a minor and disabled, I am dealing with MENTOR and your doctor telling my lawyer what to say and how to say or how to love you by saying to just write a note saying, "I love you Joshua, from Mommy". I have not been allowed to see you or hear your voice since 1999 and they know this. You don't even know what I look like or know what my voice is like and that is what they want done. Writing a note they way they dictate is something anybody can do or say and it still is another way to block any real love or bonding with a mother and child. Your stepfather, and I with your sister Joy who is sick is going to court on June 25, 2003 with your father to fight against MENTOR, Dr. Dryer, and CPS, and get the right to have home visits because of Joy being ill and being disabled, and we are fighting to get weekly phone calls. You are 12 years old and old enough to get this card and letter without it being blocked by your doctor. Jesus was 12 years old when his parents found him teaching the leaders of the church with wisdom and since Jesus is King of your heart and lives in you what make Dr. Dryer think you are not wise or smart enough to get the truth in the card and letter I send you. We pray over the gifts, cards, and letters and they are your private property for the doctor and your lawyer to save until you are 18 years old and they should be brought to the judge. I sent you cards with the Bible in it so you will not forget where you come from and who you belong to no matter what they say. You are a child of God and God has the last say. I don't believe for one minute anything I have heard from your doctor, and I am praying against it to God for God to send his angels to protect and war against them while you are in foster care. You don't have to fight in foster care and they don't have to get a police on you either. I love you no matter what and so does Jesus. We are dealing with some godless people taking care of you right now and I don't know if you are allowed to go to church but everything that has happened to you God will judge them for. You are my first born and I love you very much. Write down a diary or journal and hide it until you turn 18 years old. Write down everything you feel without telling Dr. Dryer or anybody in the foster home so when you get angry and they abuse you, you have your weapon to fight back in writing, write down what is being done to you by CPS, the courts, and MENTOR, and then that way when you turn 18 years old you can sue them and speak up for yourself. They are only lying and saying what they are doing is in your best interest because you are a minor and can not defend yourself being disabled and in foster care. It is very cruel what they are doing. I am so sorry about you breaking the windows, I am sorry they called the police on you, and most of all I am very sorry that Dr. Dryer and Ms. Animashaun never had the decent respect to treat me as your mother or contact your father to call us when those things happened to you to allow your father and I to talk to you during those times on the phone. They never even asked the judge since 1998 to 2003 for court ordered phone calls to bond with you and know what was going on directly. I never stopped praying for you and will always love you. I sent the letters to my lawyer to review because the CPS worker kept lying to you and blocking everything and I asked my lawyer to give them to you. I am sending the letters to you as a mom should because I don't know how long your doctor, Dr. Dryer, MENTOR, and Ms. Animashaun from CPS will continue to play games to do whatever they can to lie and block bonding keeping you in foster care. Last year Dr. Dryer said it was ok to have visits but they never provided transportation to see you and I was pregnant with Joy needing home visits or phone calls to bond with you. This year Dr. Dryer told my lawyer I could have visits and then she changed up writing a letter saying how bad your behavior was this year and how they fear that you would behave badly if you saw me. I asked for a phone call on your birthday with my lawyer present and they still said no. You can save my letters as you grow up. I will not stop writing what I feel in my heart to you as your mother. I will save these letters to show to the judge that I have written you and given gifts of love. They can lie and be cruel but they can't block a mother's prayers.

Love Always

Mommy

After I sent this letter to Joshua, I felt better because the Lord told me to continue to write Joshua and do exactly how I did before the devil used CPS to steal my children. I took Joshua to Sunday School, gave him church tapes from the tape ministry at United Baptist Church and from First Apostolic Faith Church to encourage my son, and so the Lord told me to do everything I did when he was with me by faith as if he never left. I have a contesting hearing on 6/25/03 which will take a miracle from the Lord. I sent my court appointed attorney and the Maryland Attorney General the following documents for my family case and all they have done is shifted the case around:

Circuit Court of Maryland for Baltimore City
110 North Calvert Street, Division for Juvenile Causes
Baltimore, Maryland 21202

IN THE CIRCUIT COURT OF MARYLAND FOR BALTIMORE CITY DIVISION OF JUVENILE CAUSES

Re:

Baltimore City Department of Social Services

VS

Crystal Dixon

Joshua Sweeney Bey
Petition Number:898170004
DOB: 6/19/1991
ID Number: 0160897

India Sweeney-Bey
Petition Number:898170005
DOB:7/7/1996
ID Number: 0172691

Linda Ann Bey
Petition Number:899224004
DOB:7/20/99
ID Number: 0180543

MOTION TO STRIKE AND CONTEST THE MENTOR NETWORK RECOMMENDATIONS (DR. DONNA DRYER, KIM ADGERSON, AND BRAXTON ANDREWS) AGAINST VISITS

Crystal Dixon, mother of Joshua Sweeney Bey, will move the court an order to strike all unconstitutional recommendations by MENTOR eliminating visitation with her son.

GROUNDS FOR MOTION:

1) MENTOR has been assigned by CPS/DSS for the care of my son under foster care contrary to Joshua getting a unbiased medical care paid by his parents (biological parents).

2) MENTOR was not court ordered by a judge for medical care and was never contested by his biological parents.

3) MENTOR have never contacted biological mother to arrange visits or alternatives for bonding such as supervised phone calls, letters, cards, gifts, or family counseling since they were assigned by CPS/DSS without a judge court order for medical care. I never got a phone call or information about the status of Joshua's care directly from MENTOR until 2002 and 2003 when I called them after I got their information from Rita Animashaun, CPS worker in 2002.

4) I have requested through my attorney, Grace Kilchenstein and through Ms. Animashaun, to have family counseling with Joshua and was repeatedly ignored from 1999 to 2002.

5) MENTOR and CPS arranged family counseling for Joshua with his father but kept me from knowing anything about Joshua directly until I went to court for the hearings.

6) I asked Dr. Dryer last year in 2002 about visits and she told me I could have visits with Joshua. I asked her about who made the recommendation of a stay away and against visits in 1999 on the court record as Joshua's psychologist and Dr. Dryer stated she didn't know who made the recommendation in 1999. I never got the name of the psychologist CPS repeatedly used against me since 1999 to block visits with Joshua. I got a certified letter from MENTOR dated May 23, 2003 against visits again contrary to what Dr. Dryer told me last year, this year, and told my attorney, Susan Kirwan, that I can have visits with my son.

7) CPS and MENTOR have not provided transportation last year or this year for visits and they have not provided a court order or a constitutional law stating that they have the legal right to recommend against visits with Joshua without due process or a trial by judge contesting the initial CPS allegations of neglect/abuse. DSS has limited guardianship of Joshua which means my rights as his parent are not terminated and I have a legal right and say against any unconstitutional recommendations by MENTOR and CPS that hinder bonding with my child.

8) I believe Joshua's behavior is because of something MENTOR and CPS is hiding due to injury while in foster care. I don't believe anything in the letter MENTOR sent dated May 23, 2003 about his behavior and I believe Joshua wants to return home but MENTOR and CPS has detained him under "the best interest of the child" clause under the color of law. I have not been allowed to talk to my child to know for myself what he is thinking for the entire 5 years he has been in foster care. I have not been allowed any bonding with my son on holidays and birthday occasions by the phone or other means of bonding than visits.

9) My entire situation has changed for the better and I want Joshua home with me with the plan changed to reunification striking all MENTOR recommendations off the record as unconstitutional and not in the best interest of the child.

WHEREFORE, the mother of the child, request a fair trial and consideration of striking MENTOR recommendations and giving the mother custody and reunification.

Respectfully

Crystal Dixon

Circuit Court of Maryland for Baltimore City
110 North Calvert Street, Division for Juvenile Causes
Baltimore, Maryland 21202

IN THE CIRCUIT COURT OF MARYLAND FOR BALTIMORE CITY
DIVISION OF JUVENILE CAUSES

Re:

Baltimore City Department of Social Services

Crystal Yvonne Dixon

VS

Crystal Dixon

Joshua Sweeney Bey
Petition Number:898170004
DOB: 6/19/1991
ID Number: 0160897

India Sweeney-Bey
Petition Number:898170005
DOB:7/7/1996
ID Number:0172691

Linda Ann Bey
Petition Number:899224004
DOB:7/20/99
ID Number:0180543

MOTION FOR DISABILITY ACCOMODATIONS FOR HEARINGS AND VISITS WITH CHILDREN

Crystal Dixon, mother of children, is requesting a court order by legal motion to have mandated disability accommodations for visits with her children and for all hearings. Crystal Dixon has had a prolonged 5 year litigation since 1998 while having her family Constitutional rights violated by BCDSS which has caused Legal Abuse Syndrome (another form of Post Traumatic Syndrome See www.familyrightsassociation.com/books under Legal Abuse Syndrome by Karin Huffer, M.S., MFT) depression in which she is on medication Lexapro, severe chest pains, panic attacks whenever she has to attend hearings and visits with the children in DSS office setting and at her attorney's office, and other physical health complications. Crystal Dixon has a disabled 8 month old infant that needs proper care at home and makes it difficult to come to any more unconstitutional, non-court ordered, un-contested visits with her children and any more hearings. All 3 of Mrs. Dixon's children were taken without contest to the initial CPS allegations of neglect/abuse before a real trial judge and a jury without any criminal charges and due process. Supervised visits were never contested by court appointed attorneys for 5 years since 1998. Supervised visits does not have to be at DSS facility and strictly without having the DSS worker supervised by video and audio tape to prevent governmental abuse.

GROUNDS FOR MOTION

1) Crystal Dixon, Joshua Sweeney Bey, and her 8 month old infant are all disabled under the Social Security Administration. We have the right as a family to have a disability attorney to the CPS case instead of a one size fit all approach with having a children's attorney by legal aid and a public defender.

2) Susan Kirwan, mother's court appointed attorney, has been given Crystal's medical information to provide for disability accommodations and Susan Kirwan insisted on asking the physicians questions violating client-patient confidentiality and trust disclosing information that I am in a CPS child custody case with my children not home instead of asking for direct medical documentation about my physical health that prevents me from coming to court and the visits. I refused to have my privacy rights violated again to get visits and proper accommodations. Susan Kirwan and I have sent emails to each other to make an agreement on a proposal for medical documentation and Ms. Kirwan insisted on discussing what she wanted to the doctors about the CPS case violating my trust and privacy. I told her I am having Legal Abuse Syndrome and health complications from the 5 year litigations and she wanted to manipulate the entire phone call and documentation to the doctors. I asked her to be on 3 way phone while I am present and she never provided the exact questions she will ask as if I am a child and not knowing my physical health and mental limitations with the court hearings and visits. Susan Kirwan has taken almost a month time to provide a proposal since I suggested medical documentation for accomodations for my health. I have had repeated communication

problems with Susan Kirwan ignoring my concerns with the case. I told her about CPS and MENTOR blocking visits and she stated that she was surprised that my son's doctor reneged on visits. I had a 6 or 7th updated psychological evaluation in Susan Kirwan's office on January 15, 2003 that would have been very favorable to my case in defense until Susan Kirwan stated to the doctor that she wanted me to plea bargain and terminate my parental rights because she felt the odds were against me. I got a 3 paged letter from her showing her doubts about the entire case and her incompetency with the case and I told her to tell the judge about her doubts and feeling uneasy about the case. She refused to state anything to the judge. I had the problem with her violating client-lawyer confidentiality when I told her I just had a baby in September 2002 and she told the master judge Koban that I had a baby making CPS to come to my home without due process ignoring constitutional rights without any written court order by judge Koban. I still have not been provided any written papers that CPS had permission to violate my rights and search my home without a warrant. Susan Kirwan failed to get this warrant or documentation. Susan Kirwan has repeatedly gone over my concerns and violated my trust in the case. This is the 3rd court appointed attorney that has done offensive things like this. It has been harmful to my health since 1998 with having 3 court appointed attorneys that are ineffective, insensitive, and continue to push me through the system worrying more about their reputations than my family rights. Susan Kirwan emailed me that she wanted the medical documentation for Rita Animashaun and I told her she need to worry about getting the documentation for the judge instead for the CPS worker as if Ms. Animashaun is the law. The judge has the final say not CPS. I gave Susan Kirwan the doctors' information and my pharmacy information with the medication I am on for depression and endometriosis and I gave her information about Legal Abuse Syndrome. She rejected all of this information and insisted on sending information to the doctors violating my privacy with the CPS case. I also told her that my daughter is too ill to take to court and the visits. I have a medical documentation from her pediatrician since January 2003 and I have proof that my daughter is on SSI disability. I told Susan Kirwan that I didn't want my daughter's medical information and privacy violated either to get accomodations.

3) My 8 month old daughter has been too ill to take out for long hours to court hearings and I will not put her in daycare disabled at this young age. I have paid for daycare before only to have the courts to postpone and inconvenience the entire family and resources for daycare to the point I would have to take my infant to the hearings risking her health and my own.

4) Susan Kirwan's office is not a fancy lower suite but more like a basement shared by other attorneys. The office is not good place for any family visit or bonding with my 3 children. It's very formal and depressing. I have gotten sick after visits in the office and my 8 month old infant has also gotten ill after visits at the attorney's office. The visit at the attorney's office has never been video taped or audio taped by the attorney for the judge and to prevent governmental abuse by CPS. This means that hearsay evidence still occurs from any visit at the lawyer's office and the judge will not be able to see for themselves how the children react and how my family bond.

5) The BCDSS CPS site for visits is worse than the attorney office. I have been treated like a criminal for 5 years instead of innocent until a judge rules me guilty or liable of the allegations which has never happened since 1998. I have to watch how I hug my children, be put in a closed room with see through windows where I am supervised, and there have not been any family outings arranged in 5 years. There has never been any video and audio tape of the worker for the visits to prevent false information and governmental abuse. The lawyers have never attended the visits from 1998 to 2002 to see for themselves how my family bond.

6) I have not been provided with transportation by DSS, or anybody else for the hearings and visits. It is a huge inconvenience to come to visits and the hearings risking my health and my infants not knowing if either one of us have to go the emergency room or the clinic after a hearing or visit. When I get sick from the panic attacks and chest pains from the hearings or visits, I am not any good to care properly for my husband or my disabled 8 month old child who needs special attention that only her mother can give. CPS, the courts, my attorney,

and any party will not pay my family's doctor bills when we get ill from the hearings and unconstitutional visits that have never been court ordered by the judge since 1998.

ACCOMMODATIONS NEEDED

1) A disability and civil rights attorney appointed for both my son Joshua and myself, Crystal Dixon as disabled citizens is need to be court ordered to balance out the case.

2) Copies of the CPS manual which is 400 pages long is needed to make sure what CPS rules were violated and what disability laws were ignored by the CPS and DSS workers.

3) Copies of the CINA manual of the procedures of the juvenile court. I was never given a written manual or explanation by all 3 court appointed attorneys, the judge, the office of public defender, DSS, or anybody to know my rights and how the entire process work since 1998 to 2003.

4) Mandatory video and audio taping of all visits in the home of Crystal Dixon and elimination of visits at the lawyer's office and BCDSS office. Mandatory home visits with Susan Kirwan (mother's attorney present), Rita Animashaun (CPS worker), a representative from MENTOR (Kim Adgerson or another social worker) Beverly McDermott (CPS worker supervisor) or another person supervising over Ms. Animashaun, and the children's attorney.

5) Have the judge provide written notarized testimony and strike physical presence of Crystal Dixon to any more court hearings. Have the judge mandate my attorney presence instead and request that all court procedures be done by phone so Crystal Dixon can hear what is going on and reply under oath by phone. There must be some court disability accommodations the judge can court order to make sure Crystal Dixon is fully aware of the activities of the court and can testify without risking her health and her infant's health.

WHEREFORE, Crystal Dixon, is respectfully requesting disability accommodations in the best interest of her children and at low risk to her health.

Respectfully

Crystal Dixon

SEE ATTACHMENT DOCUMENTATION GIVEN TO SUSAN KIRWAN ABOUT LEGAL ABUSE SYNDROME. I ASKED SUSAN KIRWAN TO USE THE DOCUMENTATION AND MS HUFFER AS EXPERT WITNESS AGAINST CPS.

Circuit Court of Maryland for Baltimore City
110 North Calvert Street, Division for Juvenile Causes
Baltimore, Maryland 21202

IN THE CIRCUIT COURT OF MARYLAND FOR BALTIMORE CITY
DIVISION OF JUVENILE CAUSES

Re:

Baltimore City Department of Social Services

VS

Crystal Dixon

Joshua Sweeney Bey
Petition Number:898170004
DOB: 6/19/1991
ID Number:0160897

India Sweeney-Bey
Petition Number:898170005
DOB:7/7/1996
ID Number:0172691

Linda Ann Bey
Petition Number:899224004
DOB:7/20/99
ID Number: 0180543

MOTION TO DISMISS SHAM PROCEEDING BASED UPON FALSE ALLEGATIONS

Crystal Dixon, mother of children, will move the court for an order dismissing the initial CPS allegations of neglect of all 3 children, demanding for CPS to expunge the allegations off the Central Registry for DSS for the reason the action is a sham and an abuse of the process of this court, and that the plaintiff's complaint is wholly based upon hearsay, lack of preponderance of evidence, and without pressing criminal charges.

GROUNDS FOR MOTION:

1) CPS allegation is that mother is unable to care for children since 1998 to present, 2003, due to lack of support systems, and mental health reports CPS obtained by threats and under duress (mental health reports dated from years before Joshua was ever born when mother was a teenager). CPS failed to take photos of injuries alleged in 1998, failed to take photos of home in 1998 of neglect, and CPS failed to summons all accusers in medical records and reports from 1998 to 2003 eliminating immunity laws which violates Bill of Rights Amendments and federal Constitutional laws to face all accusers.

2) CPS failed to have a warrant for detaining children from hospital and removal from mother in 1998. CPS failed to press criminal

charges against mother for alleged physical abuse in 1996 and in 1998 because CPS lacked evidence.

3) CPS had contract paid psychological evaluations and parenting classes done without a court order by a judge or a verdict by the judge. CPS service plans were signed under duress without proper attorney representation. CPS/DSS arranged medical care with The Mentor Network without a court order by a judge without giving the biological parents a chance to contest. CPS and MENTOR never told Crystal Dixon when Joshua started medical care with MENTOR or arranged family counseling with MENTOR. The court stipulations in 1999 stated a psychologist recommended against visits but CPS never provided the psychologist name or contact information to Crystal Dixon and the court never provided the legal right to contest medical care with MENTOR. Supervised visits were arranged without a lawyer present to and a judge never court ordered supervised visits from 1998 to 2003.

4) CPS failed to notify mother of any shelter hearing, give mother CPS manual or regulations to protect family rights in the case. CPS failed to contact attorney in reference to signing legal CPS contracts or service plans to eliminate governmental abuse.

5) Court appointed attorney failed to provide motions to fight against CPS. CPS workers wasted time from Fall 1998 to May 1999 with due process in arranging psychological evaluations, parenting classes, and requirements in biased CPS service plan arranged by CPS worker Aronda Okojie. CPS evaluations done on 10/99 and for Dr. Dale Peterson was done due to violation of due process by Aronda Okojie. DSS/CPS should have known that the same methods used by Dr. Peterson are nationally used and known for all forensic psychological testing for CPS cases. Ms. Okojie failed to use the time during parenting classes to arrange the proper psychological evaluation. CPS extended the 15-22 month rule for TPR. From the fall of 1998 to the fall of 1999 that was exactly 12 months wasted by DSS after the mother cooperated to stipulations violating Constitutional rights, and the 15 months ended before Dr. Peterson's evaluation. CPS and DSS stated to Dr. Peterson that I violated court dates and TPR rules with

the 15 months without admitting CPS worker's negligence. During this time CPS never told Crystal Dixon when MENTOR was assigned to Joshua for medical care without a court order by judge. Until Father's Day 2003 Crystal Dixon was not aware that Marvin White, Joshua's father, was allowed to have family counseling with MENTOR with Joshua, and that Mr. White knew what schools Joshua was in. Crystal Dixon, mother of children, was treated with bias by CPS and MENTOR. Mr. White, Joshua's father alleges that CPS would not allow him to have any visits without a court order by judge based on the fact he missed a family counseling session with MENTOR one time. CPS had both biological parents of Joshua in competition with each other without any court orders by a judge and violating both our parental rights. Joshua's biological parents were never contacted when he was hospitalized repeatedly or in any police trouble. We had the legal right to have our attorneys present with supervised visits or phone calls to visit or bond with our son. This issue should have been contested to the court judge to protect federal Constitutional rights and our parental rights. The visits in the hospital, the phone calls, and the visits at the DSS facility should have all been done professionally with video/audio taping or a court mediator present to prevent governmental abuse while preserving parental rights to bond.

6) CPS workers, DSS attorney, and my court appointed attorneys all stated I could not contest or plea innocent of the charges since 1998 while telling me to sign all court stipulations with the threat of reunification. There wasn't any rights or ramifications explained. Whenever I contested verbally I was told it was procedure to sign the stipulations and I would have my chance in court to rebuttal later before a trial judge. They kept doing this the entire 5 years with intimidations.

7) CPS took my children because of being on welfare, poor, having a special needs child, and being a single mother, and because of CAPTA laws that gives the State of Maryland bounties and bonuses for every foster child. Disability laws for myself and my son were ignored by CPS and the juvenile court. There were never disability accommodations or a disability attorney appointed to the mother in

defense even before being awarded SSI funding in 2001. For the allegations of low IQ, false allegations of schizophrenia by CPS, and mental illness. CPS failed to provide manuals, transportation, and provide a civil rights attorney for the mother and children. CPS took my children due to social, economical, racial, and disability discrimination.

WHEREFORE, the mother of the above stated children, demand a fair trial hearing contesting initial allegations by CPS enforcing disability laws, Constitutional laws in the US Constitution and Bill of Rights Amendments, and demand discrimination be reversed by sham proceedings.

Respectfully

Crystal Dixon

Circuit Court of Maryland for Baltimore City
110 North Calvert Street, Division for Juvenile Causes
Baltimore, Maryland 21202

IN THE CIRCUIT COURT OF MARYLAND FOR BALTIMORE CITY
DIVISION OF JUVENILE CAUSES

Re:

Baltimore City Department of Social Services

VS

Crystal Dixon

Joshua Sweeney Bey
Petition Number:898170004
DOB: 6/19/1991
ID Number:0160897

India Sweeney-Bey
Petition Number:898170005
DOB:7/7/1996
ID Number: 0172691

Linda Ann Bey
Petition Number:899224004
DOB:7/20/99
ID Number: 0180543

MOTION FOR TAINT HEARING

Crystal Dixon, mother of children, moves the court for an order to have a taint hearing to challenge investigative interviews of the children by BCDSS attorneys, CPS workers, social workers, psychologists, GAL, and the children's attorney.

Joshua is to be 12 years old which is old enough to speak for himself in a court of law at the TPR and CINA hearings. All children should have been audio and video taped during visits to prevent governmental abuse and false CPS reporting/documentation.

See attached "Taint Hearing: Issues for Forensic Psychologists" document for the motion for Taint Hearing.

Crystal Dixon believes all 3 children have been violated of constitutional rights and wrongfully influenced by the foster parents, CPS workers, social workers, MENTOR program for Joshua, and the children's attorney with intimidations along with false questionings.

WHEREFORE, Crystal Dixon, urges the court to dispute and contest wrongful cross examination, interrogations, and negligence by authorities detaining all 3 children under duress and in violation of their fundamental Constitutional rights as US citizens by means of thorough aggressive review taint hearing to preserve the civil rights of the family.

Crystal Dixon, mother of the children, request and urges the court to have Joshua appear in the court for himself and have taped testimony of India while being brought to the TPR and CINA hearings. The children are of age to know right from wrong and can testify in the court of law with age appropriate questions to allow the judge to see in the court how CPS has wrongfully influence the children.

Respectfully,

Crystal Dixon

Circuit Court of Maryland for Baltimore City
110 North Calvert Street, Division for Juvenile Causes
Baltimore, Maryland 21202

IN THE CIRCUIT COURT OF MARYLAND FOR BALTIMORE CITY
DIVISION OF JUVENILE CAUSES

Re:

Baltimore City Department of Social Services

VS

Crystal Dixon

Joshua Sweeney Bey
Petition Number:898170004
DOB: 6/19/1991
ID Number:0160897

India Sweeney-Bey
Petition Number:898170005
DOB:7/7/1996
ID Number: 0172691

Linda Ann Bey
Petition Number:899224004
DOB:7/20/99
ID Number: 0180543

MOTION TO COMPEL PRODUCTION OF DOCUMENTATION TO PROTECT DISABILITY RIGHTS AND CONSTITUTIONAL RIGHTS

Crystal Dixon, mother of children, moves the court to enter an order compelling CPS, the Office of Public Defender, and Juvenile Court CINA office to provide a copy of each agency's policies and procedures manual requested by 6/6/03.

Said documents are necessary to assist mother of children in working with CPS, CINA, and OPD. These documents were never provided by a court appointed attorney, CPS, or the juvenile court system to explain the court procedures and polices and to make sure CPS follow their own manual and regulations. Due process, disability rights, and federal constitutional laws have already been violated by CPS, the OPD, and the court system by not producing written explanations of the laws on court stipulations, by not providing written policies that respect federal disability laws, and not having a disability attorney assigned to the case to Joshua Sweeney Bey and Crystal Dixon who are both labeled by the Social Security Administration as disabled citizens. There has never been any written manuals or documents as stated above provided from 1998 to 2003 to the mother of the children and the court appointed attorney. The court appointed attorney and the court system pushed Crystal Dixon and the case through the system without any accountability, any proper due process for a disabled family, and ignoring federal constitutional laws. Crystal Dixon is requesting a motion to compel production of these manuals for effective and aggressive protection of her family's fundamental constitutional rights. See attachment of emails as proof that there is a CPS manual of 400 pages. I have requested the complete 2000 pages of discovery the DSS attorney gave my attorney and I was told I had to pay $250 for my own life. I asked my attorney, Susan Kirwan repeatedly to review the 2000 pages and have been ignored for months. I asked Rita Animashaun since 2001 for copies of the entire CPS file with her case notes so I can review them and I was ignored. I am making a motion to compel the 2000 pages of discovery and the CPS workers' file/notes and reports from 1999 to 2003. I am asking for the court to waiver the fees or costs of getting the manuals and documents requested in this motion due to the fact I am disabled and on limited income. I am asking for copies of the case and the manuals under the FOIA Act which enables me to have copies free.

Respectfully,

Crystal Dixon

It is now June 25, 2003 the day I had to appear for the contesting hearing for all 3 children (Joshua, India, and Linda). My husband, Joshua's father, and myself were all there with my 9 month old infant Joy. The DSS attorney used Dr. Dryer from MENTOR as an expert witness. My attorney failed to prepare me for the case or hearing that day and when we came to court she stated she would cross examine about some issues but when the time came she failed to do anything she stated to me before the hearing. Dr. Dryer testified to diagnosis and reports that were never told to my attorney or me since 1999 and it was traumatic to hear as a mother all of the negative statements by Dr. Dryer. Of course she dictated that I write a note saying just "I love you, from Mommy" which I believe is another loophole. I told the judge it was my first time ever hearing any of the statements by Dr.

Dryer and I contested before the judge several lies that were made by Dr. Dryer. Judge Mahasa court ordered that DSS give me through my attorney progress notes of Joshua's behavior. However, Judge Mahasa court ordered the dictated note which I believed was very insensitive to the trauma of hearing the testimony by Dr. Dryer. My life was put on hold by CPS as if I was guilty for 5 long years and all Judge Mahasa kept saying to me was that it didn't matter what I wanted and all I kept hearing in my head by the judge was, "It is not about you. It's about the best interest of the child!" So why prolong the case if they can not provide a time frame and change the permanency plan to reunification because of Joshua's special needs. Once they steal your children in foster care you rights are terminated so that meant my rights were terminated in 1998! We found out in court that Joshua is on 5 or 6 different medications which upset me greatly. My husband and I prayed about the matter. My husband and I still want to file a civil lawsuit against the State of Maryland and CPS for how constitutional laws and disability laws were violated for 5 years. The entire matter has affected my physical health to the point I was fighting hospitalization. I contacted the Maryland Disability Law Center to persuade the public defender to use disability laws. I sent MENTOR and my attorney an electronic American Greetings Card online so that they can screen it on their own without having me waste money on stamps and expensive cards only for them to reject it. Here's the documentation about the card I sent for Joshua:

Subj: **This is to verify you got Joshua's court ordered card! FROM CRYSTAL DIXON**
Date: 7/3/2003 11:59:25 AM Eastern Standard Time
From: Blessed Crystal
To: kirwanlaw@erols.com

I will forward this to Braxton Andrews. Please give this to Rita Animashaun and use this as court evidence that I obeyed the order under duress. I need to know the next step of the loophole MENTOR is using to block real bonding now. I will also forward this to Kim Adgerson so she will have this email as court ordered evidence for the 6 month review hearing on 12/8/03 for Joshua. The court order made me physically sick last week and my husband and I are not in agreement with Judge Mahasa's decision for any court ordered dictated communication. Unfortunately we can not get a private attorney to appeal and we both do not trust you, Susan Kirwan, as a court appointed attorney. We do not want another court appointed attorney for the appeal against Judge Mahasa's court order due to do repeatedly having 3 incompetent court appointed attorneys including yourself. We feel that you should have gotten reports from MENTOR before the hearing last week and you failed to prepare my husband and I for the case or hearing which was legal negligence and total insensitivity. It was shocking to us both and to me as a mother to hear those negative things about Joshua without being told since Dr. Dryer was paid by DSS or CPS and assigned by DSS for medical care in 1999. I asked Dr Dryer who put the stay away order or blocked visits since 1999 and she stated she didn't know. I still need to know was psychologist made this stay away order. If you and MENTOR have a problem with the cards I sent and email I sent last week please arrange a phone conference with MENTOR by 3 way or have MENTOR write you another certified letter before the next hearing ASAP. I will give you the documentation that Joshua's name is Bey and not Sweeney. It is up to Joshua to change his name to Sweeney.

Sincerely

Crystal Dixon, mother of Joshua Sweeney

Subj: **Your Greeting was just picked up**
Date: 7/3/2003 9:14:02 AM Eastern Standard Time
From: zach@americangreetings.com
To: blessedcrystal@aol.com
Sent from the Internet (Details)

The Greeting you sent to braxton.andrews@thementornetwork.com on 07/02/2003 23:03 was just picked up.

To view your Greeting, choose from the options below.

Crystal Yvonne Dixon

Click on the following link.
http://www.aol-aol.americangreetings.com/view.pd?i=328206059&m=3410&source=aol-aol999

OR

Copy and paste the above link into your web browser's "address" window.

OR

Enter the following Greeting Number, 03282060593410, on our Greeting Pick Up Page at
http://www.aol-aol.americangreetings.com/findit.pd?source=aol-aol999

If you have any comments or questions, please visit
http://www.aol-aol.americangreetings.com/customer/emailus.pd?source=aol-aol999

Thanks for using AmericanGreetings.com.

Subj: **Your Greeting was just picked up**
Date: 7/3/2003 11:17:58 AM Eastern Standard Time
From: zach@americangreetings.com
To: blessedcrystal@aol.com
Sent from the Internet (Details)

The Greeting you sent to kirwanlaw@erols.com on 07/02/2003 23:03 was just picked up.

To view your Greeting, choose from the options below.

Click on the following link.
http://www.aol-aol.americangreetings.com/view.pd?i=328206057&m=3410&source=aol-aol999

OR

Copy and paste the above link into your web browser's "address" window.

OR

Enter the following Greeting Number, 03282060573410, on our Greeting Pick Up Page at
http://www.aol-aol.americangreetings.com/findit.pd?source=aol-aol999

If you have any comments or questions, please visit
http://www.aol-aol.americangreetings.com/customer/emailus.pd?source=aol-aol999

Thanks for using AmericanGreetings.com.

It is July 2, 2003 which is the day CPS is suppose to TPR my rights of my girls. I had to get two doctor slips from my GYN doctor and my internal medicine doctor to excuse me from court. I went on July 1, 2003 to see my GYN doctor and was told I had to get surgery for endometriosis and she wrote a note excusing me from court. My husband insisted that I still go to court on July 2, 2003 to get a documentation from the judge of postponement. When I got there with my baby Joy, you could have bought Ms. Animashaun, the CPS worker, for 5 cents and so they postponed the TPR to September 22, 2003. My attorney, Susan Kirwan, still insisted on giving me a hard time and when I got home my husband said that they are not God and that I don't have to keep explaining stuff to them. My spiritual mother said that she believes that they are trying to get me locked up, put in a crazy mental institution, and charge me for contempt of court. She told me that the devil is a liar because he actually thought he would wipe me out and shut me up. So the 6 month review hearing for Joshua that was contested on June 25, 2003 is scheduled to December 8, 2003 and they are going to attempt to terminate my rights of my girls, Linda and India, on September 22, 2003. So it will be 6 years I have been fighting the CPS system and the courts. I tell you, there has got to be somebody out there in the world I am going through this testimony for to encourage, because I just don't believe your tests and trials are just for you. I believe as someone is reading this book they have gone through worse than I have and need to hear that a little nobody like me who was a social reject still endured, still praise the Lord, and still survived with faith in God.

It's July 23, 2003 and I am still going through with Susan Kirwan, the court appointed attorney, with the issue over the court ordered card for Joshua. Here are the e-mails about the court ordered card:

Subj:	**court order on 6/25/03 states**
Date:	7/21/2003 1:16:59 PM Eastern Standard Time
From:	Blessed Crystal
To:	kirwanlaw@erols.com

The court order states:"The BCDSS shall submit progress reports to the parents (mother's through her attorney Susan Kirwan, Esquire) reqarding respondent's therapy and education. Mother and father shall reestablish contact with respondent as recommended by respondent's psychiatrist beginning with a card stating" I love you from mommy and/or daddy." It doesn't state anything like in the email you sent us! We can send the card to the judge or to Dr. Dryer through you. The court order is not specific and in the specification form we sent MENTOR, you, and Dr. Dryer! Anything will bug Joshua out, the court order made the card a legal document and dictated under duress, and it's not from me. I can not as a Christian lie. You need to photocopy the card or email we sent you for your file that it was sent and when on 7/18/03. We still have not gotten Joshua's progress notes as court ordered!

Subj: **Re: copy of Joshua's card**
Date: 7/21/2003 12:03:06 PM Eastern Standard Time
From: Kirwanlaw@erols.com
To: BlessedCrystal@aol.com
Sent from the Internet (Details)

Dear Mrs. Dixon:

I am not sending a copy of your correspondence to Judge Mahasa for her signature. That was not part of the court order. The court order was that you were to send a card to Dr. Dryer for delivery to Joshua. You have mailed a copy to Dr. Dryer, and you have therefore substantially complied with the court order.

Very truly yours,

Susan Kirwan

Subj: **Request Joshua to have written communication**
Date: 7/17/2003 7:58:10 PM Eastern Standard Time
From: Blessed Crystal
To: kirwanlaw@erols.com

You have photocopies of notes Joshua sent me through Rita Animashaun by MENTOR. I want Judge Mahasa to court order that MENTOR allow Joshua to weekly write me since he has done it before. There should be a taint hearing with Joshua present to allow the judge to ask Joshua if he want to write his mother weekly and send cards. The cards should all be presented to the judge on the record that Joshua is writing his mother and I should get all his cards and communications in court and not through CPS or MENTOR. The cards all need to be on the court record. The issue with the court ordered card is abusive and manipulative and there should be a court order for Joshua to communicate in writing if he can write and wants to write me. Joshua's school teacher should be there summons to court and bring copies of Joshua's handwriting to prove that he have and can presently communicate in writing. Joshua should be allowed to send me drawings of how he feels and should be allowed to write his mother on a weekly basis. I am being abused as to how to show love to my son but the judge and MENTOR didn't say anything about allowing Joshua to write his parents to express his emotions and feelings. I think it will be theraputic instead of having MENTOR unjustly due to Joshua's alleged medical condition court order his parents what to say and do. All of the communications will be sent to the judge to review that is written by Joshua to have on the record. So even though Joshua is writing on a weekly basis Mentor will have a folder for the judge with all of Joshua's writings to put on the record for the judge to review his progress and his feelings first hand.

This is a good strategy against MENTOR and CPS.

Sincerely

Crystal Dixon
Subj: **Re: Urgent email for MENTOR**
Date: 7/17/2003 12:47:48 PM Eastern Standard Time
From: Kirwanlaw@erols.com
To: BlessedCrystal@aol.com
Sent from the Internet (Details)

Dear Mrs. Dixon:

If you do not wish to spend money on a card for Joshua, I would suggest that you print out one of those pictures (any one of those pictures would be a good choice) and then write with a pen as follows:

Dear Joshua:

I love you.

From,

Mommy

Do not put anything else in the note. Do not notarize it. You recall Donna Dryer saying in court that all you should put was something simple like that. The notarization would be too complicated, and I believe that Mentor and Dr. Dryer would not give him anything with a notarization.

You received the correspondence from Andrew Braxton. He said that he would not send any e-mail correspondence to Joshua. He said that Joshua would want something physical that he could hold in his hand.

Dr. Dryer will be out of the office until August 16, 2003, so I will not be able to speak with her until then.

Very truly yours,

Susan Kirwan

WHAT IT REALLY WAS LIKE TO BE A JEHOVAH'S WITNESS, BY CRYSTAL DIXON

I was born into the Jehovah's Witness faith by both my parents who were devout Witnesses. I recall having a green Witness Bible in my hand at age 3 years old and I could not even talk well stuttering like crazy. I would stutter so badly I would bang on something to talk. I knew I could not celebrate my birthday, holidays, and associate with anybody that was not a Witness as soon as I could talk and was a toddler. I was going from door to door with my parents in the cold weather, rain, snow, and practicing how to get people to take the Watchtower. All of my friends were Witnesses. Being a Witness was difficult for me because all I wanted to do was please my parents. When I became a teenager at age 14 I got baptized which was the exact same age my mother got baptized as a Witness. Then I became a regular pioneer which in the Witness faith is dedicating 90 hours a month to ministry. What Witnesses had to do was report how much time they used going from door to door, street witnessing, and other ventures to get more members into the Witness religion. I was very smart in school and was on the honor roll from the 8th grade up to the 12th grade. I wanted to go to college but my parents and at the time the religion was against college. This of course made my guidance counselors and teachers upset that I could and would not pursue scholarships and take advantage of my high grades from high school. After high school I got a job and met my first boyfriend and I was a virgin. Despite being molested as a child and what the doctors put in my medical records, I never allowed any man to penetrate me. The doctor broke my hymen at the clinic when my mother took me to get a physical for a yeast infection because the doctor didn't believe I was a virgin as a teenager. When I graduated and got a job, I started sneaking out the home to be with my first boyfriend who was not a Witness. Then I was finally excommunicated from the Witness faith for fornicating. I didn't have anything but the clothes on my back. My mother was abusive to me before I got baptized as a Witness physically and mentally. One time she sent me to school with a black eye and my science teacher asked me to report her but I was too afraid. After loosing childhood friends, family, and all support systems I became promiscuous looking for love in the wrong places from being in a religious cult and being abused by my mother. I never did drugs while in the world. I got drunk once and never did that again. I never smoked cigarettes either. I kept making foolish decisions in my life with abusive men. I was pregnant with Joshua homeless in the House of Ruth, a shelter for battered women, and I got my first place alone with Joshua August 1991. Off and on I would return to the Kingdom Hall to see my family and have some support for Joshua but they were not allowed to talk to me because I was dead and that was their capital punishment in the Witness faith. Doesn't this method sound like CPS and how they play God? To cut you completely off from your family and friends was just as cruel as CPS taking my children. So you can imagine raising a special needs child alone and dealing with my own self worth and insecurities. I was a walking target and carried a chip on my shoulder all the time. Now that my parents got a divorce on July 2, 2003 and my mother almost got disfellowshipped just like I was, I can only pray for my family to be saved and come into real Christianity. Everything I did was in my mother's footsteps and I try extra hard to fight that. I was separated by my family at age 18 and CPS took my children. Some things I have learned to forgive myself for and I try to heal completely. I know one thing being a Witness and Moslem instilled some discipline. There were some things I would never do no matter how desperate I was. When I got excommunicated in 1989, I was homeless and then I went into Job Corps to try to get my life together on my own. I left Job Corps and months after I was raped while on my period by an African man. My mother didn't believe that I was raped and when I went to the hospital she brought up issues about me leaving home with my first boyfriend. However, when things started showing up that I was raped she wanted to hurt the man. I had to go to the rape crisis center and my counselor was Levita Christian. She said that if I didn't reply to the rapist the way I did I would have been killed. Then for years I would have nightmares and flashbacks of the rape. Whenever I would come on my period I would really have a difficult time. So then after I was raped I went into computer training school where I met Joshua's father. I stayed with Joshua's father and he was abusive to me, I got pregnant and had an abortion with his child, and months later got pregnant again with Joshua with his father still abusing me. So that is when I went into the House of Ruth shelter for battered women pregnant and that is how I got my first apartment. You would think I would learn not to get involved with any more abusive relationships, NOT. I got involved with a Moslem man and he was cheating on me with a woman in the Moorish temple after proposing to marry me. I had a nervous breakdown and the ministers from the Moslem temple came to see me in the hospital. Then I got into another relationship with the man I thought was my soul mate and the man I had the longest relationship with, Charles Batten. Before him I thought sex should be painful and he was the first and only man I know to make me have a real orgasm. Not even my husband can cross those lines and I love my husband. That is just like the devil, you wait to get married and you get a Holy Ghost filled man that can't get it right in bed, my husband is my heart and I love him but sometimes I have to fight thinking about my relationship with Charles. Charles and I keep breaking up and getting back together for 5 years and even now after he knew I am married he still tries to get back with me. There's a part of me that still care about Charles but I would never go back. In between my relationship with Charles I had an abortion and Charles even now brings up that I killed his baby. Back then when I told him about our baby, he drove me to the abortion clinic and said it was not his out of fear of responsibility. I had a third abortion from a one night stand during the times Charles and I broke up. I would go back and forth to the Kingdom Hall and church trying to find the Lord and at the same time get support. I believe not having a strong father figure in my biological father and a very abusive mother caused me to keep settling for anything in relationships. It wasn't until I actually got filled and baptized with the Holy Ghost in 2000, I finally had the Comforter and inner support I needed to the point I didn't need to be co-dependent on anybody but Jesus. Being raised a Jehovah's Witness took a lot of my youth by not being able to go to my junior and senior prom, not doing social stuff that normal teenagers do, and constantly dealing with low self esteem. Now I don't want anybody to think being a Witness was all sad stories and bad. I had some very good times in my childhood. What I miss about being a Witness is that there is no such thing as like in these churches where you can not get one on one help from the pastor because the membership is so large, on the contrary, Jehovah's Witnesses make sure the congregations are split up and the elders come to your home and do what I call "house calls" to make sure you don't sin or do anything wrong against the rules. Jehovah's Witnesses have Bible Study or what they call "Book Study" in an elders' home or a member's home and that is close fellowship other than the regular weekly congregational meetings. Another thing I miss about being a Witness is that they have their own dress code, you can tell a Witness a mile away, just like you can tell a Moslem a mile away. What gets me upset about the church is that you can't tell the world from the church and no matter rather you are Baptist or Apostolic, the American churches do whatever and however they want. Christianity is a culture not just a Sunday church thing! Just like public schools have a school uniform, which they didn't have when I was in school in the 1970's and 1980's, I believe churches should have a dress code. Another thing I miss about being a Witness is that I did more traveling as a Witness than I do now. My mother would have people from Mexico and different people come into our home that were Witnesses. I never forgot a lady from the Netherlands stayed in our home. My mother also made sure as I grew up that I had some type of culture so she made sure I went to take ballet lessons and tap dance lessons. I saw The Dance Theatre of Harlem, my mother took me to see musicals and plays, and as a result I could sing. I was always in some talent show singing. When I got saved I was in the choir and even now I can sing but I am hesitant to sing in a choir after being wounded at United Baptist Church. So what I do now is write poems and write songs in a book to stir up my gifts. I love to sing songs of Zion especially when I am feeling depressed and have nowhere or nobody to talk to for an answer. That's when the Lord would put a song in my heart in the middle of the night or early in the morning and that song will last me all day or stay in my spirit for that week. What I don't miss about being a Witness is that they believe only a limited number can partake Communion which is to them 144,000 of only Witnesses and the rest that is only Witnesses have to pass the Communion around. When I got saved and took communion for the first time in the church it was a beautiful experience for me because I was taking the blood and body of Christ inside of me and after all the hell I been through in my life whenever I took Communion I felt washed and redeemed by the Lord. When I think back about how I was raised as a Witness and what happened to my life, I still count it all joy.

TO BE ABLE TO BREATHE AGAIN – PART 4

To be excommunicated by my parents, family, friends as a Jehovah's Witness at age 18 I though was the end of my life. To have a special needs son at the age of 20 years old without any support systems as a single parent, I thought was difficult and at times I wanted to throw in the towel. When my children were taken from me by CPS in 1998, I thought it was the end of the world. To have 3 abortions, one miscarriage, and 4 live children, I thought I was a whore and God would never forgive me. When my children were taken I thought at first it was punishment for having children out of wedlock and the 3 abortions. When I was raped I thought I was being punished. Especially when a man raped me on my period and said Jesus would bless me after he took it. I thought I was cursed. But God has revealed to me all the miracles and grace he has on my life. I can finally breathe again spiritually and naturally. There is no condemnation any longer. I don't have the fear or worry any longer looking over my shoulders. Total surrender to God is now in place. The peace of God reigns in my life, Hallelujah! God has turned the pages of my life and changed the script. It's not about being married but the fact that I am God's woman and precious to Him. God is my protection full of compassion and mercy. Terminating my rights of my children is a great sacrifice but it's out of my hands. God has supplied all my needs for 5 years after my children were taken and he kept me in my right mind without being in prison those 5 years. I am a walking and talking miracle thanks to the hand and power of God! Who shall I fear, the Lord is my strength of my life and whom shall I be afraid, the Lord reigns forever and He is Lord. Praise the name of Jesus. God has so much in store for my life and he will use my life for his glory as a testimony for others. I pray people see nothing but Jesus in my testimony and get strength to endure and praise the Lord no matter what comes their way. Glory to God!

ABOUT THE AUTHOR

Mrs. Crystal Dixon is born and raised in Baltimore, Maryland. She is an advocate under American Family Rights Association for Maryland at www.familyrightsassociation.com/members/maryland/index.html. She is also an ordained minister authorized by Pastor Fred Nech at United Christian Faith Ministries, 304 South 6th Street, Osage City, KS 66523 Voice: (866)888-3944 Fax:(760)923-7779. She is a high school graduate at Paul Laurence Dunbar Sr. High in Baltimore, Maryland and she completed two years of college with an Office Supervision Certificate at the Community College of Baltimore County-Dundalk campus. She is the mother of 4 children:Joshua Sweeney, India Sweeney-Bey, Linda Bey, and Joy Dixon. Crystal Dixon is a woman of deep faith and resilience who has overcome so many obstacles with the power of God. She wants to help others be encouraged through reading this book.

www.ingramcontent.com/pod-product-compliance
Lightning Source LLC
Chambersburg PA
CBHW020336290526
45785CB00005B/2050